The IEA Health and Welfare Unit

Choice in Welfare No. 53

Adoption: The Continuing Debate

Patricia Morgan

Commentaries:
Felicity Collier
Conna Craig
Chris Hanvey
Karen Irving
Barbara Ballis Lal
Liv O'Hanlon
Jim Richards
Richard Whitfield

IEA Health and Welfare Unit
London

First published October 1999

The IEA Health and Welfare Unit
2 Lord North St
London SW1P 3LB

ISBN 0-255 36456-3
ISSN 1362-9565

Typeset by the IEA Health and Welfare Unit
in New Century Schoolbook 10.5 point
Printed in Great Britain by
Hartington Fine Arts Ltd, Lancing, West Sussex

Adoption: The Continuing Debate

Contents

The Authors

Patricia Morgan, Senior Research Fellow at the IEA Health and Welfare Unit, is a sociologist specialising in criminology and family policy. Her books include *Delinquent Fantasies*, 1978; *Facing Up to Family Income,* 1989; *Families in Dreamland*, 1992; *Farewell to the Family?*, 1995; *Are Families Affordable?*, 1996; *Who Needs Parents?*, 1996; and *Adoption and the Care of Children*, 1998. She has contributed chapters to *Full Circle, Family Portraits, The Loss of Virtue*, *Tried But Untested*, *Liberating Women from Modern Feminism*, *Just a Piece of Paper?* and *The Fragmenting Family,* as well as articles for periodicals and national newspapers. Patricia Morgan is a frequent contributor to television and radio programmes and is presently writing a full-length work on the relationship between capitalism and the family.

Felicity Collier has been Director of British Agencies for Adoption and Fostering (BAAF) since August 1995. Qualifying in social work in 1978, she has worked in childcare social work, family court welfare and the probation service as practitioner, training manager and assistant chief officer. She was a guardian ad litem for several years and obtained her M.Phil in social work in 1994 at Brunel University and the Tavistock Clinic.

Conna Craig is President and a Trustee of the Institute for Children, Inc., in Boston, Massachusetts (US). She has advised politicians and opinion leaders on practical steps to restructure adoption and foster care, and is profiled in Robert Danzig's *The Leader Within You* as one of 34 of America's successful leaders. In 1997 she was named by *Policy Review* as one of America's 'New Social Architects'. In 1996 Conna Craig was awarded the first annual Salvatori Prize for American Citizenship; the Salvatori Prize recognises 'extraordinary efforts by American citizens who are helping their communities solve problems the government has been unable to solve'. She has spoken in the US and the UK to audiences of economists, clergy, policy makers, state budget officers, philanthropists, private and public child welfare providers, foster and adoptive families and children. She graduated with honours from Harvard College.

Liv O'Hanlon has been a journalist for 25 years and has worked mostly in newspapers, but also in radio, television, and publishing, both in Australia and the UK. She has had a long interest in social affairs which was heightened by her first personal involvement in adoption about ten years ago. She and her husband now have two children from overseas. After writing many articles on the state of adoption, she was compelled by frustration and the calls of similarly-minded people with professional or personal interests in adoption to set up The Adoption Forum, a pressure group, in October 1996. She and the management committee are always eager to hear from those who are keen to aid and abet their cause.

Chris Hanvey is Director of the John Ellerman Foundation and is here writing in a personal capacity. He was formerly Director of the Thomas Coram Foundation and before this a director of NCH Action for Children. He has held senior positions in several local authorities, mostly in the area of childcare and currently chairs the adoption panel of a very busy London borough.

Karen Irving is Director of Parents for Children. She has had over 26 years of experience as a social worker, 15 of them in adoption and fostering. She has had several articles published in the specialist press, and was elected a Fellow of the Royal Society of Arts in 1994.

Barbara Ballis Lal is Associate Professor In-Residence in the Department of Sociology, UCLA, Los Angeles, California. She teaches courses in sociological theory, political sociology, and convenes a special topic seminar on 'The "Chicago School" of Sociology: the Historical and Comparative Study of Race and Ethnicity in Cities'. She is currently doing research on how theories and concepts, such as that of ethnic identity, influence and are invoked by professionals in the formulation and justification of policies and programmes regulating adoption in the USA and Britain.

Jim Richards is Director of the Catholic Children's Society (Westminster) and has spent most of his professional life involved with children and family work. He regularly makes written contributions to the debates on adoption and is co-author of guides to aspects of adoption.

Richard Whitfield, an Emeritus Professor of Education with a background in both the natural and social sciences, has senior voluntary sector experience in social work management. Now a freelance consultant he hosted three formative consultations on adoption during his period (1993-97) as Warden of St George's House, Windsor Castle. Two of his family's four now grown-up children were adopted in babyhood in 1965 and 1977.

Foreword

The plight of essentially parentless children is one of the thorniest of all public policy issues. These are children whose biological parents have been deemed unfit, unwilling or unable to raise them. In terms of the passion which this debate engenders, it is in a category with Europe, 'aid' to less developed countries, the National Health Service and capital punishment.

It is also of academic interest, or perhaps I should write an academic puzzle, for two reasons. First, it is hard to think of any other subject on the policy agenda where there exists a deeper ravine between the views of the public and the views of the so-called 'experts'.

Second, it is hard to think of any other subject where there is: (a) so much confusion and ducking and diving regarding the statistics but (b) once the numbers are finally forced out into the open, the data on children in pain are so utterly stark and all point in just one direction, namely adoption.

On a recent radio programme, for example, an MP stated that adoption was very, very successful. He claimed that only 50 out of every 2,000 such arrangements failed, i.e. a success rate of 97.5 per cent. Against him was a very senior and prominent social worker who immediately countered that adoption has a success rate of only 50 to 60 per cent. I suspect both are right on their own terms, but that the former is counting harvested apples while the latter is trampling on apple blossoms.

The MP is talking about real actual adoptions that have been done and dusted, signed and sealed, approved and finalised by the courts. The social worker is talking about departmentally-approved adoption *plans*. For example, local authority A suggests placing child B with family C. That's The Plan. For some reason it does not come through to the final legal conclusion of formally adopting the child. So it counts as a failure even if child B ends up totally happy with another family and Family C successfully adopts a different child. To the MP that's two victories and to the social worker that's multiple failures: hence the discrepancy in their claims.

Designing From Scratch

But imagine you were starting from scratch to design a childcare system. Just think about a few, basic, fundamental questions you would need to answer:

- Who should be responsible for taking children in danger away from their abusive, neglectful, biological parents?
- What training should these child 'takers' have?
- What criteria should the child 'takers' use in removing a child?
- To whom should these 'takers' be held responsible?
- Having taken a child, where should they place the child and for how long?
- Under what circumstances do the 'takers' return the child to a biological relative with a history of abuse or neglect?
- If a return is not possible then what?
- And for how long and where?

These are really tough questions needing clear, principled, child-rooted answers rather than the PC motivated nonsense that pervades many parts of the childcare system of today.

A Tripartite Problem

To understand what is going on here you have to break the problem into its three component parts.

First, there is the flow of children entering the foster-care pool. Who are they? At what rate are they entering? What age/sex/race etcetera are they? Why are they entering? How do they compare with previous generations of entrants: older, younger, or what?

Now you have this pool of 50,000 plus children. What are their overall demographics? How long have they been in that pool? How many moves have they been forced to make? How many are legally free to be adopted right now, and for how long have they been so free to be adopted? How many have been returned to their families only to be re-abused and readmitted into the system? Why do the data differ so widely between different authorities? Think of those 50,000 plus as you go to sleep tonight.

What is happening to these children? How many are ever returned successfully to their families, broken down by, say, age and length of time in the system? How many never return home and eventually 'age-out' of the system at 18, or even younger? And of those who do 'age-out', how many are homeless, how many are in prison, how many are on benefit, and how many have what we generally consider to be a happy life?

We have to do three things. First, we have to staunch the flow of children into the system. Second, we have to limit the time the children spend in the system. Third, we have to ensure the children move on with reasonable speed to permanent loving homes whether it be back to a biological relative or on to adoption. This problem is not only about today's 50,000 plus kids and two billion pounds a year of taxpayers' funds but also about the increased downstream costs to the welfare and prison budgets as a direct result of the failure of the state to take care of them.

Finally, I remember a line I heard in a speech some years ago by Conna T. Craig, one of the contributors to this volume. Herself a foundling turned foster kid turned adoptee turned graduate of Harvard College turned President of the Boston-based Institute for Children, she tells her audiences: 'No child is unadoptable and no child should turn 18 in the system'.

No child is unadoptable: no matter what the circumstances, there is a family willing to adopt every child. Indeed, there are long lines of families willing to adopt children of all ethnic backgrounds, of all ages, and with every type of disability. Perhaps the most public example of this in the UK is the former MP Peter Thurnham who adopted a child who is both physically and mentally disabled. No child should turn 18 in the system: in other words no child should be allowed to graduate out of the system rootless, without a permanent loving family.

Getting It Into Context

The backdrop to this whole debate is, of course, the breakdown of the family, a breakdown aided and abetted by governments of both main parties and a breakdown which has seen births to single mothers double every decade from roughly eight per cent at the start of the seventies to 16 per cent at the start of the eighties to 32 per cent at the start of the nineties, to 35 per cent today. The marginalisation of adoption and the encouragement of single mothers has, of course, dried up the source of healthy babies we are wont to think of when adoption is first mentioned in polite company. Coupled with this has been the vogue among social workers over the past 25 years for family preservation, that is the view that no expense should be spared in reunifying the abused or neglected child with its parent(s) even when there is a very high chance that the kid will be quickly back in the system.

The results are horrifying. All of the 'pool' of 50,000 plus above have first of all been abused or neglected to such an extent that even today's social workers, whose expected standards of care are not high, have felt compelled to take them away. Next they languish in local authority care, being at best frequently moved around to prevent 'bonding' or at worst further molested in some way. (The scandals surrounding child abuse in local authority children's homes have been stacking up to such an extent in the last few years that it is difficult to keep track of them.) They become 'system' kids.

What does finally happen to these children? Imagine you are director of social services today—right this very minute—for a major urban area and you have 1,000 children of a range of ages in your care. What will happen to those kids, that pool of 1,000, over the next say 10 to 15 years? Forget (just for a moment) the flow of new kids entering every day; focus only on that group of 1,000 you have now, today, under your control. Based on conversations with childcare professionals over many years, here is how it will, in my view, probably pan out: 200 will go home, suffer more abuse or neglect and rapidly re-enter the system—more below on these children; 400 will go home and be successfully reunified with their family of origin (this number is artificially high because it includes a number of kids who are in the system overnight say as a result of a car accident to the parents); 210 will enter some form of kinship care, that is, long-term paid care by a relative, or be assigned to long-term foster care; 100 will stay in the system and will 'graduate' out on reaching majority or will simply run away; 80 will either be adopted or come under some form of guardianship; and for ten we don't know and never will know. (Some of Fred West's victims were 'care runaways' who were never missed—until their remains were dug up.)

Now let us return to the first group, the 200 who were sent home; who were re-abused and who re-entered the system. What will happen to them? Some will go home many times. One young lady I know was taken away nine times and sent home eight times before she was two. At the end of the day I predict: 50 successfully returned home; 40 into kinship or long-term foster care; 100 graduate out/run away; and for another ten we will never know. Claims that one-third of the homeless and 40 per cent of the prison population are ex-system kids are at first startling and barely credible, but on reflection make sense.

The State As Parent

The state makes a lousy parent and parenting is one more business the state should leave to the private sector.

For six years the IEA has been highlighting the scandal described above. Through an ongoing programme of lunches, lectures, dinners and briefings at 2, Lord North Street, we have attempted to inform public debate on this issue.

A key element in this area of our work was the publication in March 1998 of *Adoption and the Care of Children: The British and American Experience* by Patricia Morgan. It outraged some while propelling others to even greater efforts at reform. It became the keystone to a sustained effort by newspapers (in particular *The Daily Mail, The Express, The Guardian, The Independent* and *The Evening Standard*), politicians (in particular Julian Brazier MP and his all-party group but also notably the Rt Hon David M. Davis MP, The Rt Hon Jack Straw MP and Paul Boateng MP) and others such as our authors to expose the problem, analyse its reasons and suggest reforms.

At one of the many meetings that followed the publication of *Adoption and the Care of Children*, Robert Whelan, Assistant Director of the IEA's Health and Welfare Unit, and I hatched the idea of challenging a range of senior figures in the field to write 5,000 words each about the Patricia Morgan book. We wanted to create an extended discussion, if you like, of her analysis and her proposals. So this is a book about a book and is, I believe, a 'first' in the Institute's history. Some of those we challenged refused for a range of reasons. The eight who responded have, however, given us a very worthwhile set of papers. As with all IEA publications, the views they express are their own and not those of the Institute (which has no corporate view), its Trustees, Advisers or Directors. We hope, however, to stimulate a more informed debate which will contribute to the well-being of society's most disadvantaged children.

John Blundell
General Director, IEA

Editor's note

The contributors to this volume were asked to respond to Patricia Morgan's book *Adoption and the Care of Children: The British and American Experience*, published in March 1998 by the IEA Health and Welfare Unit. All citations in their chapters refer to this edition. The first chapter of the present collection represents a summary of the main points of Patricia Morgan's book. Readers who are interested in a fuller exposition of any part of her argument are referred to the full-length work, which is available from the IEA.

Acknowledgement

This book has been produced with the generous support of the Earhart Foundation.

Adoption and the Care of Children
The British and American Experience
(Condensed Version)

Patricia Morgan

---

1. THE PREJUDICE AGAINST ADOPTION

ADOPTION has fallen out of favour. Adoption is portrayed as being anti-child, anti-woman, and anti-black, redistributing children from the poor to the middle class.[1] Women are seen as compelled to give up children because of the way in which the male-dominated family is purportedly supported by the welfare state.[2] In what the author of the strikingly titled book *Death by Adoption* calls violent, political acts of aggression against women,[3] they are rendered powerless by the narrow-minded stigma attached to illegitimacy and the refusal of society to provide the resources necessary for them to bring up children successfully on their own.

With professional opinion turning against adoption as a strange, even repellant, practice, it tends to be excluded from the list of possibilities presented to women with problem pregnancies and childrearing crises. If the mother raises this uncomfortable subject, it may be passed over by telling her to 'have the baby then see how you feel', with the hope that she will be reconciled to keeping the child. Counsellors do not simply proceed on the assumption that pregnant adolescents have little or no interest in adoption, but provide little or no support for those who might want to explore this.[4]

Thirty years ago there was a stigma attached to having an illegitimate or unwanted child. However, '[a] single woman who brings up a child today may be applauded as independent and strong; the stigma has passed from the unwed mother to the mother who relinquishes her child'. In this hostile climate: 'the revelation that a woman gave birth to a child before marriage is scarcely shocking. It is much more difficult to explain why the baby was adopted'.[5] The result is that: '[w]hereas previously there had been heavy social pressure on unmarried mothers to decide on adoption, they were now more likely to be pressurized in the other direction'.[6] It seems that social workers cannot deal with the idea of women putting a child up for adoption and have difficulty accepting their decisions.[7]

Table 1

Numbers and Percentages of Children Leaving the Care System via Adoption 1981 -1998

	Total number of children who left care	Children adopted out of care	% of children who left care through adoption
1981	38412	1636	4
1982	37408	1828	5
1983	36409	2044	6
1984	34238	1912	6
1985	32793	1920	6
1986	31611	1935	6
1987	30688	2038	7
1988	30678	2301	7
1989	28917	2316	8
1990	29070	2478	9
1991	28282	2439	9
1992*	14100	1080	8
1993	32000	2500	8
1994	32100	2300	7
1995	32500	2100	6
1996	32100	1900	6
1997	30800	1900	6
1998	29300	2000	7

* Figures for 1992 cover 14 October 1991 to 31 March 1992 only, owing to the implementation of the Children Act in 1991.

Figures for 1994 - 1998 exclude children looked after under an agreed series of short-term placements.

Figures have been adjusted to compensate for local authorities where it is known that more than one per cent of records were missing due to unresolved discrepancies in the data or incomplete returns.

Source: Department of Health, *Children Looked After by Local Authorities, England*, various editions.

Figure 1

Adoptions and Baby Adoptions, England and Wales, 1975 - 1997

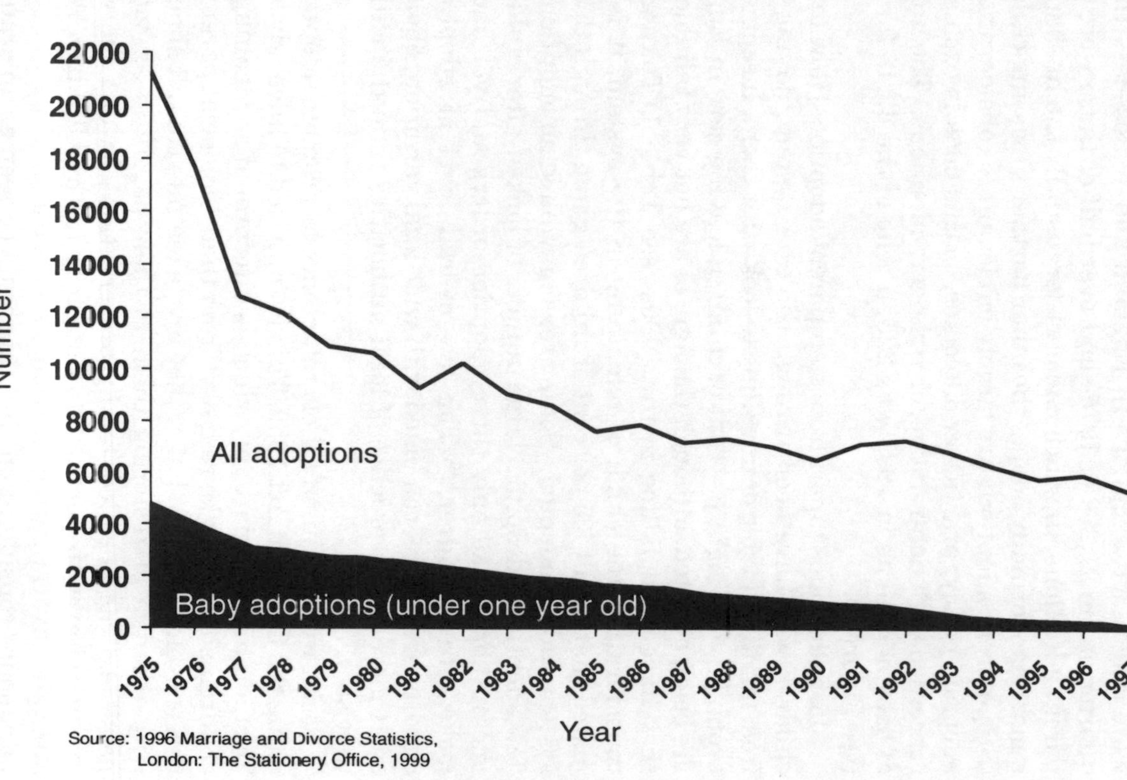

Source: 1996 Marriage and Divorce Statistics, London: The Stationery Office, 1999

Unsurprisingly, in this climate of opinion, there has been a steep fall in the number of adoptions taking place. In 1997 there were only 5,306 adoptions in England and Wales—less than a quarter of the 21,299 of 1975—and over half of these were step-parent adoptions, in which one partner (usually the husband) in a marriage formally adopts the other partner's existing children. (Step-parent adoptions are largely irrelevant to considerations of adoption policy, practice or outcomes, so this book is exclusively concerned with non-relative, or stranger, adoptions.) The number of baby adoptions in 1997 was 225, a relic of the 4,548 for 1975 (see Figure 1).

Most adoptions (apart from step-parent adoptions) now involve children who have been through the care system, having come from families unable or unwilling to look after them. It seems that around five to eight per cent of children leaving care in England are being adopted, although the figures are not very reliable, and they have been falling in the 1990s (see Table 1).Taking into consideration the children remaining in the system, it is estimated that about 3.5 per cent of children going through the care system end up adopted.[8] Some areas may have no adoptions,[9] or 'few adoptions, despite a large number of looked-after children... one authority had only three adoption orders and yet had 457 looked-after children'.[10] The low overall level of adoption of children from care, combined with wide local variation, obviously owes more to the practice of local authorities than the children they serve.

Social workers justify their reluctance to promote adoption by citing the Children Act,1989. This is supposed to have advocated 'partnership with parents', which is interpreted as meaning that children should not be removed from their biological parent(s) if this is avoidable, and that, if they are taken into care, it should be with the aim of restoring them to their parent(s) as soon as possible. This is called 'family preservation'. In fact the words 'partnership with parents' do not occur in the Children Act. It strongly advocates that 'the child's welfare shall be the court's paramount consideration', but this could be seen as an argument *for* adoption rather than against it.

The lack of enthusiasm for adoption on the part of local authorities is made more serious by the fact that they are almost the only players on the field. The Adoption Act, 1975, followed by the Seebohm reorganisation of social services departments at the end of the 1970s, gave local authorities a virtual monopoly over adoption. The number of voluntary agencies handling adoption has more than halved since the 1960s, and those that remain work in close co-operation with their local authorities, with the exception of the small number of baby adoptions.

2. THE OUTCOMES OF ADOPTION

The hostility towards adoption is difficult to understand when we consider its success as a response to the needs of children who cannot live with their biological parents. Adopted children do well by many indicators. However, before we look at the statistical evidence, we need to ask ourselves with whom we are comparing adopted children. The obvious answer would be with children of the same social class and general background as the adoptive parents. However, as a stable home with their biological parents is not on offer for these children, this would be 'comparing apples and oranges... the only *bona fide* comparison is to youth raised in settings that would have been the destiny of adopted youth had they not been adopted'.[11] The '*bona fide* comparison' here, then, is with children reared in residential care, fostered, or restored to their biological parent(s) after a spell in local authority care.

The British Agencies for Adoption and Fostering (BAAF) estimates that the breakdown rate of adoptions averages around nine per cent. These include children suffering from major disabilities or multiple problems and school-age children.[12] For those aged under two, the breakdown rate is under five per cent—rising to 12.8 per cent for the six-to-nine age group and to 14.2 per cent for the over-tens. Not surprisingly, the younger the child at placement, the lower the risk of breakdown.[13]

Babies are, of course, the easiest to place and easiest to parent. More typical of present-day adoptees are the children in a major study of 1,165 'special needs' placements made by voluntary agencies for local authorities in the early 1980s.[14] A small number had one special need, mainly Down's syndrome, while 84 per cent had eight or more, whether being seriously ill, institutionalised, having behavioural or emotional problems, and so forth.

Overall, 21 per cent of their placements had broken down within a period of between 18 months and six-and-a-half years, making 79 per cent successful–being almost identical to the one in five recorded in other prominent studies.[15] Rates of breakdown were highest for children who had experienced multiple moves in the care system prior to adoption, for children who had been in institutions, and for children who had experienced deprivation or abuse.

The Outcome of Early Adoptions: The Adopted Baby as a Child

Most studies of adopted children until the 1980s were of early adoptions.[16] All the children born in a particular week in 1958 in the UK have been subjects for the periodic follow-ups of the National Child Development Study (NCDS). These included a study of birth status, involving 366 illegitimate children who had not been adopted and 182 illegitimate children who had been adopted, as well as those children born in wedlock.[17] On the whole, those adopted as babies tend to do well compared with children in general, but not always quite so well as the biological children of families in similar circumstances.

At age seven, the adopted children were better readers than either the legitimate or illegitimate children, being about ten months ahead of the legitimate who, in turn, were 14 months ahead of the illegitimate children. They were as good at arithmetic as the legitimate children and better than the illegitimate. When it came to social adjustment, a slightly higher proportion of the adopted (16 per cent), compared to children of married parents (13 per cent), were rated as maladjusted, although a quarter of those born illegitimate were in this category.

At 11 years of age,[18] one in three of the illegitimate children was living with a lone parent or in 'other situations': one in six had been in care and one in three families was receiving public assistance. (One in ten of the legitimate children was no longer living with both natural parents.) The illegitimate children living with both natural parents, as well as with one parent, or a step-parent, also tended to live in poorer circumstances than the legitimate children. In comparison, the adopted children were continuing to live in 'exceptionally favourable circumstances'. Very few had experienced family breakdown, only four per cent of families received public assistance, and both middle- and working-class adoptive families usually maintained or improved their circumstances over time.[19]

Adopted children were still likely to be better readers, on average, than either legitimate or illegitimate children from the same sex, class and family size. Only when all environmental variables *were considered together* did the differences diminish significantly, as we might expect. Allowing for all background conditions, adopted girls had the highest, and illegitimate girls and adopted boys the worst maths scores for the children's groups. Adopted boys seemed to have made less progress in this area between seven and eleven compared to other groups in similar conditions.

At 11, the born-illegitimate children again showed the poorest social adjustment according to ratings made at school, and the difference with the legitimate was only slightly reduced when allowance was made for environmental factors. However, background factors made a bigger difference for the adopted children, so that these were less well adjusted on average than legitimate children when allowance was made for their relatively more favourable home environment. It seemed that the behaviour of the adopted had deteriorated relative to the other children between seven and eleven. A similar change in behaviour ratings of adoptees between ages five and ten has emerged from reports of another cohort of UK children born in 1970.[20]

The Adopted Infant In Adolescence And Adulthood

The Search Institute of Minneapolis undertook the investigation of adoptees in adolescence, using the largest-ever sample of adoptive families in the United States. This involved a total of 881 youngsters, aged 12-18, adopted as babies between 1974 and 1980, their parents, and non-adopted siblings. The research used a plethora of psychological and family measures, many of which were specially developed for the project, and also used a national USA sample of 47,000 adolescents for comparison, and a matched school sample.

Over a half of the adopted youth were highly attached to both parents, and absence of attachment to both parents characterised less than two per cent.[21] Overall, 70 per cent of adoptive parents reported that their children's attachment to them was strong or very strong. Only eight per cent reported weak or very weak attachment. In turn, 95 per cent of parents felt strongly attached to their adopted child, and 88 per cent reported a high level of emotional closeness. The percentage of adopted adolescents reporting high self-esteem (55 per cent) was higher than in the national sample of adolescents (45 per cent), and there were no differences between adopted and non-adopted siblings. Adopted adolescents were far less likely than adolescents in general to experience parental divorce or to live with lone parents.[22] The adoptive families were also marked by higher educational attainment, family income above the national average, and a stronger connection to religious institutions.

There were far higher levels of parent/child communication and parental involvement in schooling for adopted adolescents, compared to the national sample. Indeed, for positive parent/child relationships, warmth, discipline, positive communication and parents as a social resource, the adopted sample exceeded the levels shown generally and more or less matched the levels for non-adopted siblings. In terms of factors important for children's well-being, adoptive families seem to accentuate the positive and minimise the negative factors. There was a near unanimous agreement from parents (96 per cent) that adoption has been a rewarding experience, although one in five said it had created marital stress.[23]

The Search Institute paid particular attention to whether their adopted adolescents showed raised rates of difficult behaviour or other problems of adjustment. According to indicators of psycho-social well-being related to the successful navigation of adolescence, the adopted adolescents did at least as well as and often better than youth from a general sample. Of course, the adopted sample had experienced less divorce and separation, had a higher average family income, and higher parental educational attainment. However, adopted youth also did as well as non-adopted siblings in the same families.

For nearly all high-risk behaviours (covering drug-taking and alcohol consumption, sexual activity, truancy, criminal behaviour and so forth) rates for adoptive adolescents were lower than for the general sample. A relatively high percentage of adopted adolescents had received counselling or therapy (34 per cent), although most of these were not in the psychological danger zone (only 27 per cent of those receiving help were in the clinical range). However, it was on the independent mental health assessment that more of the Search adopted adolescents fell into the clinical and borderline ranges than was the case for the national adolescent sample, particularly for problem behaviours—or 15 per cent compared to 11 per cent. There may have been underestimations of symptoms in the general population, but the results are in line with other reports of somewhat higher psychiatric disturbance in adopted samples.

For the British National Child Development Study (NCDS), the illegitimate 16-year-olds had the highest rates of difficulty overall, according to school ratings, even after allowances were made for material and social factors. While the difficulties of the adopted group fell between the illegitimate and the legitimate, the apparent deterioration in the adjustment of adopted children between seven and eleven did not continue into adolescence. Indeed, difficulties had clearly peaked by late childhood and were much less marked in adolescence. Moreover, while the high overall scores of the illegitimate for disturbed behaviour reflected a wide range of problems, the restless and anti-social scores of the adopted differed little from those of the legitimate, and they mainly showed significantly greater problems in their relationships with peers.

By the mid-teens, the illegitimate children were by far the most likely to have been separated completely from their homes and to have spent time in care. As in earlier studies of the group, they were also most likely to be in families receiving state benefits and 'for many... the picture is one of continuing material disadvantage and an increased likelihood of family instability'.[24]

The Adopted Baby As An Adult

Lois Raynor's *The Adopted Child Comes of Age* looked at the long-term outcomes for adoptees, aged 22- to 27-years-old, who had been born between 1948 and 1951 in England and Wales.[25] The families involved had either fostered a child whom they later adopted, or had adopted directly.[26]

Seventy per cent of these adopted adults had made a good or excellent life-adjustment, and something like 34 per cent had acquired higher educational qualifications. Only six subjects were very badly adjusted, and five of these had not only shown difficult behaviour when growing up, but had been fostered first by their adoptive parents. Virtually none of the adoptive parents who had fostered first saw any advantage in this, and many saw serious disadvantages. They had only done it because they could not adopt directly due to their age or the existence of natural children.

The message from the UK's National Child Development Study[27] is not substantially different. Its 23-year-old adoptees had done well academically and vocationally; over 80 per cent had some formal qualifications, compared to just over 75 per cent of the legitimate group. The born-illegitimate group fared worse, as it had at every other sweep, where over half of the women and 30 per cent of the men had no formal educational or vocational qualifications at all. Illegitimate women showed the greatest vulnerability to depression and the highest rates of relationship breakdowns. Both sexes in the illegitimate group were more likely to be parents by 23; to have prolonged unemployment spells; and (in the case of the women) to have had a rate of unwed teenage pregnancy around treble that of either the adopted or born-legitimate groups.

Late Adoptions

Children who are adopted 'late'—i.e. at five years old or over—can tell us much about the capacity which children have to become members of new families. They can also tell us the extent to which a change of environment can counteract the effects of deprivation, abuse and an unpromising genetic endowment.[28]

Alfred Kadushin's landmark study in 1970 involved 91 families with children adopted between the ages of five and eleven. The children came from family backgrounds which included alcoholism, psychosis and mental deficiency; they had often been removed from cruel or neglectful parents, and had 'failed' in one or more foster homes.[29] The time it took to get them into adoptive placements meant that they had spent an average of three and a half years in foster care, and a third had three or more placements each. The children had shown an average of three specific, identifiable behaviour problems.

However, the breakdown rate for adoptive placements was nine per cent. After six to ten years, when the average age of the children was nearly 14 years, children with exceptionally unhappy and disturbed early childhoods brought at least some satisfaction to around three-quarters of their adoptive parents, as well as having stable and permanent homes. The level of success matched that for infant adoptions. However, the more behavioural disturbances shown by the child, the less likely was the outcome to be favourable.

In Victor Groze's four-year analysis of subsidised adoptions, arranged by the Iowa Department of Human Services in the 1990s,[30] the children were placed from infancy to eleven (at an average age of nearly five) and had been in their adoptive homes for an average of five and a half years. Over a half were known or suspected to have been sexually abused, and 76 per cent to have been physically abused. A half were in special classes for learning disabilities, and 15 per cent were in schooling for the mentally retarded or behaviourally disordered. A significant proportion had behaviour problems during all four years, with a half of the parents reporting an increase in difficulties. Children with a pre-adoptive history of sexual abuse seem to be particularly traumatized: 40 per cent had attention problems, 50 per cent had social problems, nearly 30 per cent were withdrawn and around a quarter had problems with anxiety/depression or offending.

Yet, over the four years, about 90 per cent of parents claimed to get on fairly well with their adopted children, and 80 per cent each year reported being close, with positive attachment in the majority of families. The 78 per cent who had reported adoption impact to be mostly or very positive in the first year had declined to 69 per cent by the fourth year, but 90 per cent had not thought to end the adoption, and over 60 per cent would recommend adoption to others. No family dissolved the adoption, although eight per cent of children ended up in out-of-home placement, usually with major behavioural problems or developmental difficulties.

Similar results have been found in other recent US studies of adoption outcomes for severely maltreated children, where the majority showed significant behaviour problems, although most families were satisfied with the adoptions.[31] This was in spite of the fact that these were samples composed almost exclusively of children from the very worst backgrounds.

It cannot be expected that children will be 'cured' after a few years; the question is more one of whether and by how much they have improved. Sometimes the answer is a great deal. A boy 'placed at eight, and thought to have severe learning difficulties, now goes to college at 17 with GCSEs'. Another 'very successfully adopted at 15 by the same family, was a normal baby, but battering left him very disabled' yet, now 'in his mid-20s he is functioning remarkably well'.[32] In a small but long-term study of 21 children placed by the Children's Society,[33] more than half had been abused or neglected before going into care, and 11 were over ten when placed with permanent new adoptive or foster families. After five years, when the children ranged from six to 20, the adjustment of nearly two-thirds was improved or much improved, and only one had lower well being. Indeed, 67 per cent were rated as having at least average or above average well-being. In 15 placements all members of the new family were satisfied or very satisfied and the children were considered attached or fairly well attached. In 81 per cent of cases the children themselves were completely satisfied, or satisfied with reservations, about their new families.

The Late Adoptee As An Adult

If there have been few studies focusing on the outcome of late adoptions, ones on late adoptees as adults are rarer still. After all, adoption after babyhood was uncommon and discouraged up into the 1970s.

A major exception is the Scottish study of John Triseliotis and James Russell,[34] involving 44 late adoptees as adults (average age 24), together with a sample of 40 people who had been reared in institutions run by statutory or voluntary organisations from before ten years of age until 16 (they had spent an average of 11 years in institutions).

The adopted were 'hard to place' children born in the 1950s, who, between the ages of two and eight, were settled with families and had been in care for an average of two and a half years.[35] A foster-care group, who had lived with a single foster family from at least the age of nine until 16, was also studied. The natural parents of the children had been overwhelmed by social and personal problems. Their turbulent relationships were usually the immediate reason for the child's reception into care, particularly as these involved many separations and desertions. In many of the families there was heavy drinking and/or a history of criminality. Two-thirds of the children who went on to become adopted were in care when under a year old, compared to only one in eight of those who grew up in institutions. Continuity was frequently interrupted, with one child having experienced 11 moves before being placed. Both groups averaged nearly four moves between reception into care and final placement. The residential group experienced further moves within what was supposed to be their permanent 'home'. They may have been held back from adoption or fostering because of the presence of siblings or a tenuous link with their original family. Almost two-thirds of the adopted were described as having moderate to severe emotional and behavioural problems (compared to a fifth of the residential group).

They ended up adopted because of the perseverance of adopting couples, or because the agency saw the adopters as being 'marginal' like the children–in which case they would not be too bothered about poor heredity or adverse early experiences. There were more lower-class adopters in this study than is usual, which reflects the way in which agencies, especially voluntary ones, were more likely to pick higher-class adopters for babies from 'uncomplicated' backgrounds.

While 86 per cent of those who grew up adopted described their relationships as 'very good' or 'fairly good', compared to 60 per cent who grew up in homes, it seemed that 'real enthusiasm for growing up in residential care... was very rare'.[36] Only 15 per cent described relationships in homes as 'very good' compared with 45 per cent of adoptees. When asked about their total experience of growing up adopted or in residential care, 82 per cent of those adopted and 55 per cent of those who grew up in homes expressed very or fairly positive feelings.

While the residential group started out with significantly fewer behavioural and emotional problems compared to those going to adoptive families, only one-third of the adopted, compared to 70 per cent of those growing up in homes, had problems in childhood. Indeed, the emotional, behavioural and psychiatric problems of the residential group trebled. (This figure is almost identical to the rate of neurotic and anti-social disorders reported by other researchers for children in long-term residential care.)[37] During the adoptive placement and before leaving school, 14 per cent of the adopted and 35 per cent of those who grew up in homes were referred for psychiatric help.

Where there was dissatisfaction with adoption, this tended to centre on intense pressure from high status parents to achieve educationally—a point to which we shall return. However, while a greater proportion of adoptees referred to 'unreasonably high expectations on the part of their parents', this needs to be balanced against the way that more of the residential sample 'commented on the total indifference of some of the staff to their future'.[38]

Adoptees achieved marked upward social mobility compared with their natural parents. Many in the residential sample achieved higher social ranking than their biological family. However, for the adoptees, there was no difference in social mobility between those who came originally from the most disturbed or disadvantaged backgrounds and others from less deprived circumstances. Both groups contrast with the children who grew up in long-term foster care, since these hardly achieved any upward generational mobility—a dismal result considering the circumstances of the original families.

While nearly two-thirds of the adopted expressed outright satisfaction with their life as adults, only 20 per cent of those who had been reared in homes thought the same way. Overall, twice as many people who grew up in homes reported problems as adults compared to those who grew up adopted—whether in terms of dissatisfaction with marriages, police warnings, appearances before an adult court, and other indicators.

Not only do adopted people fare better in every way compared to children restored to natural parents or relatives, but even when adoptees from the worst possible backgrounds are considered, their outcomes were significantly better than those for institutionally-reared people. While there tends to be a high genetic predisposition to social maladjustment and mental illness among adopted people, a stable home and the high level of careful parenting usually found in adoptive families provides a protective factor. Using the best parents for problematic children, adoption 'may mitigate, although perhaps not eliminate, the elevated risks of social and psychiatric problems in adolescence associated with children from high risk biological family backgrounds'.[39]

Why Adopted Children Do Well

Adoptive children may often be 'harder to rear' when compared to their non-adopted siblings. However, adoptive parents are more resourceful than others, well prepared for parenthood and have greater personal and social resources—being 'the only parents in our society who have to "prove" their ability to be good parents' before undertaking the task.[40] Adopted children do well because the parents are so keen to rear a child. Alfred Kadushin identified the factors in the success of late adoptions as lying in the satisfaction parents got from their relationship with the child, their mutual identification and the occupation of parenthood itself as a lifelong interest. This gave satisfaction in helping a child grow and develop, through the successful navigation of the problems of childrearing, and the appreciation of the simple pleasures of life.

To say that human beings have a tremendous ability to overcome early disadvantages must not be taken as implying that neglect, abuse or physical deprivation are harmless. Moreover, it is commonly found that: 'the older the child at placement, the more likely is it that problems will develop'.[41] Rates of maladjustment, especially if these involve serious conduct problems, are likely to rise with age at adoption and in proportion to the adversities the child has endured in the pre-adoption years.[42]

Every year adds to problems. In one study comparing adopted children referred for psychiatric treatment with those who had never used such facilities,[43] it was noticeable that the average age of the clinical group at adoption was 33 months, while that of the non-clinical was 15 months. In turn, 29 per cent of the clinical sample had a history of abuse, compared to 18 per cent of the non-clinical sample. Similarly, depressive and manic symptoms in adult adopted males have been associated with events in the first two years—even after controlling for any significant relationships with genetic background and adult substance abuse and anti-social personality.[44] The disruption involved in late placements interacted with biological predispositions to make adult disturbance more likely. The message is that: 'Children cannot be put into cold storage while adults argue about what to do for them or pay attention to the needs of other adults'.[45]

Part Of The Family?

Even when it is accepted that adopted children may enjoy many advantages, compared with similar children who were not adopted, the claim is made that none of these can compensate for the loss of a secure sense of belonging and relatedness, since, having been severed involuntarily from their original family and their roots, they cannot really become part of another family.

However, a sense of detachment or estrangement from the adoptive family is not something which comes over from studies of adopted children. Adopted people overwhelmingly consider their adoptive parents as *their* parents, and the ones that matter. The natural family occupies an insignificant place in the pre-occupations and concerns of even later, 'high-risk', adoptees.[46]

It has been claimed that adopted people are disadvantaged because they lack the knowledge of the past which makes the present intelligible, and gives the continuity so important to the formation of the self. However, this argument against adoption overlooks the fact that 'late' restorations to the natural family may be more problematic for the child than placement with a new family, due to the likely ambivalence of parents about having the child return to them, as well as changes to the family itself while the child has been in care.[47]

In Barbara Tizard's sample,[48] whether late-adopted or restored children took to parents or not depended on how much their adoptive or natural parents really wanted them, and were prepared and able to spend time with them. While the extent of parent/child activity in adoptive families was much greater than in most middle-class homes, the natural parents of restored children played with them less and encouraged them less than working-class parents. They expected restored children to be as independent as working-class children of the same age, while adoptive parents accepted and dealt with the child at his or her level of development which, for older adoptees, was often retarded.[49]

Moreover, what coherent picture of their past and future do children possess who can make no stable relationships with committed adults and who grow to adulthood affiliated to no-one, and without a base to which they can return? Children in institutions and foster homes ask 'Why am I in care?' and 'What will happen to me?'. It is they who are most likely to have trouble coming to terms with their past, and to be looking towards a troubling future. The adopted have a family caring for them, with supportive relationships in which to invest. In comparison, residential people tended to be haunted by feelings of rejection: 'I felt unwanted and rejected by my parents... they didn't care about me, that's why they put me in a home'. Children growing up in care may have as little or even less information about their original families than the adopted. Four out of five of those who grew up in homes in one study maintained that their circumstances were hardly, if ever, discussed with them: 'often being unaware whether their parents were alive or dead, or whether they had siblings or not'.[50] One person described how: 'you couldn't understand how he could be a brother and you hadn't seen him in your life before'.

Many residential people are reported to be 'particularly bitter and critical' about institutions.[51] They felt that the experience had 'spoiled' and 'wasted' their childhood and was a blight on their adult lives. It was they who saw themselves as different from others; as having had no parents and having lived excluded from normal society. Such an overwhelming sense of alienation, rejection and inadequacy affected few adopted people. For them: 'it seemed to have no meaning because, as many put it, they were wanted by their adoptive parents'. Some remembered living in institutions, but they much preferred the 'opportunity to grow up with people who wanted them'.[52]

It is curious that adoption should be perceived as such a threat to identity, when it is institutions which have been so clearly identified with this role in modern social theory—even defined in terms of social death.[53] The identity of children growing up in institutions is negatively affected by ignorance about their personal history, the absence of significant, close relationships, and the feeling that they are perceived as 'worthless'.

None of this is to deny that adoption does have its ambiguities, even when totally accepted by society, and that these centre around the way that the child does not share the adoptive parents' ancestry. However, it is interesting that similar claims about threats to identity, as well as the other adverse consequences attributed to adoption, are hardly ever made about children produced through reproductive technologies—whether egg or sperm donation, or surrogacy. When these fears are raised about adoption, we are probably witnessing a feminist position on women's rights masquerading as concern for children's identity.

Colour Blind?

There are few areas of the adoption debate which are more controversial than trans-racial adoption, or the adoption by parents of one racial group (usually white) of children from another group or groups. It has been described as a form of: 'exploitation—in that black babies and children, the most valuable resource a community has, have been taken away'.[54] As black and mixed-race children are over-represented in the care system,[55] and there is a shortage of black or mixed-race couples presenting as adoptive parents, the mis-match can cause some children to become 'stuck' in the system. Childcare professionals have become increasingly dogmatic on the issue, preferring to abandon the possibility of adoption altogether for a child for whom adoptive parents of exactly the same racial profile cannot be found.

With the black identity question at the heart of the case against trans-racial adoption, the argument is that:

> Black children growing up in white families grow up with a very confused sense of themselves. They feel white but they are regarded by the outside

> world as black. They experience racism as a black person and, however well-meaning a foster parent, there is no way that a white person can have that experience of racism or provide positive role models.[56]

The black identity or 'black consciousness' which the white adopter is incapable of nurturing is linked to 'coping mechanisms'. These arise out of the 'black experience', or the indignities and sufferings inflicted on black people, and are generationally transmitted. White adoptive parents cannot satisfy the 'psycho-survival needs' of the black child, because they cannot pass on tendencies towards doubt and the suspension of trust which black people employ when faced with racism. According to a guide for *Explaining Adoption* to your child: 'The black child in a white family is not only a minority in society but in their own family'. All in all, trans-racial adoption is blamed for leaving black children unable to cope in a black world and unacceptable to a white society, or marginalised pariahs to both.[57]

In spite of this, investigations involving trans-racial adoptions all show that they seem to enjoy much the same degree of success and satisfaction as same-race adoptions. Neither does there appear to be evidence of higher breakdown rates for trans-racial placements as the proportion of special-needs and older children have grown.[58] Whatever their race, the same factors help adopted children adjust well—lack of delay in placement, love and security in the family, good relationships with adoptive parents, siblings and other relatives, as well as an open, relaxed approach to appearance and background.

Trans-racial adoption in the USA was investigated in the early 1970s using groups of 44 trans-racial adoptions involving a black child and 44 white couples with a child of their own race.[59] According to both the parents' and investigators' reports, there was no difference between the two in the high levels of satisfaction.

Soon after, another study reported on 125 trans-racially adopted children who had lived with their adoptive families for an average of seven years. At nine years of age the picture was of predominantly well-adjusted children, living with parents who were very satisfied with their adoption experience. The success rate of 77 per cent was much the same as that of other studies that had looked at white baby or older child adoptions.[60] Similar adjustment rates of three-quarters or more have been obtained on both sides of the Atlantic from follow-ups of trans-racial placements.[61]

It was noticed in *Adoption and Race,*[62] a report on the families of largely trans-racially adopted children with an average age of 14, that the study children were doing better academically than their age-mates. Barbara Tizard had previously found that mixed-race children adopted by white families were the most intellectually gifted of the adopted children, with reading attainments generally above average, while their problem scores did not differ from those of white children.[63] This is underscored by results from other studies conducted in the USA at about the same time, which reported significantly higher IQs for adopted black children compared with the average for black children and for those reared in their birth-homes.[64]

In Barbara Tizard's research, some of the most unhappy children in the least successful placements (by any criteria) were mixed-race or black children restored to a reluctant natural parent at the insistence of social workers. Another study reported much the same a few years later when it compared 27 mixed-race adopted children with others in care or being reared by lone mothers. Even in relation to white adopted children, and white children at the same schools, the adjustment of the trans-racially adopted children was excellent.[65]

But Are They Black?

In an attempt to comes to grips with how adopted black children see themselves, Rita Simon and H. Altstein assessed racial awareness in families, each of whom had adopted at least one non-white child as a baby or toddler (which involved 388 children between three and eight years).[66] They found that trans-racially adopted children actually had a much more accurate and positive perception of their race than other black children. At the same time, they were more indifferent to race as a basis for evaluation than any other group reported in any previous study on children in the USA, Hawaii, New Zealand, and other parts of the world.[67]

One hundred and thirty three of these children were followed up at 11.[68] Around 20 per cent of the adopting parents described problems relating to the children. One (which occurs with same-race adoptions) was the 'rather painful discovery that their adopted children had physical, mental, or emotional disabilities that were either genetic, or the result of indifferent or abusive treatment... received in foster homes'.[69] Another problem was that the children born into the family sometimes felt left out because the family had changed its lifestyle so much (in terms of churches, schools, holidays and so on) to meet the needs of the inter-racially adopted child. However, most of the parents reported that the adoption had brought happiness, commitment and fulfilment into their lives, being the 'wisest and most satisfying decision they had ever made'.[70] In turn, 74 per cent of thc adopted children were doing well in school and appeared to have no difficulties. As a group, the children themselves were not only more comfortable about their own racial identification, but also more racially 'colour blind' or indifferent to race as a way of evaluating people.

Barbara Tizard's findings also indicated that trans-racial adoption, far from inhibiting black children from acquiring an accurate and positive image of themselves, was more likely to encourage that process, without race becoming a prominent issue. It was the children restored to their biological parents who showed more confusion and negative feelings about themselves.[71]

There are no 'studies which support the fears of black social workers about the dangers of trans-racial placements'.[72] Bans or barriers to inter-racial adoption exist not only regardless of the disproportionately high numbers of black children in care who need a permanent home, but despite the findings of research, and the traditional principles of childcare. It means that 'instead of race being treated as one factor in deciding on the interests of the child, thc child becomes a factor in deciding on the interests of the race'.[73]

3. THE ALTERNATIVE TO ADOPTION - 'CARE'

Adopted children have far fewer problems than non-adopted children from similar birth circumstances—whether we are talking about early or late adoptions, whether we ask adoptees or adopters, and whenever in the childrearing cycle we ask the questions. Adoption is 'perhaps the most therapeutic of all therapies',[74] the most successful form of preventive intervention or rehabilitation for children from disturbed backgrounds. Insofar as anything works, only a permanent substitute family seems up to the task of bringing troubled children to adulthood. However, the most probable response to the needs of children who, for whatever reason, cannot live with their biological parents, will be to rear them in the public care system.

There is little doubt that care children are the most disadvantaged of the child population. They suffer in terms of their education and their physical and psychiatric health. Care-leavers account for less that one per cent of their age group, but they are massively over-represented amongst the disadvantaged. More than 75 per cent leave school with no qualifications—a rate which is 12 times higher than that for children in general.[75] Only between 12 and 19 per cent go on to further education, compared to 68 per cent of the general school population. Between 50 to 80 per cent are unemployed: fourfold the rate for youngsters between 16-24.[76] In turn, 23 to 26 per cent of adult prisoners (depending on the sample) and 38 per cent of young prisoners have spent time in local authority care before 16, as have 30 per cent of young, single homeless.[77] Overall, care children are 60 times more likely to join the ranks of the homeless and 50 times more likely to be imprisoned. The statistics are similar in the US where 40 per cent of the children leaving the system end up on welfare, and between 23 per cent and 39 per cent of homeless youth are former foster children, who also make up nearly 14 per cent of America's prison population.[78]

Investigations of ex-care populations all conclude that many are not only retarded in their emotional and social development as children, but also in adulthood.[79] Michael Rutter and colleagues[80] studied nearly 100 men who had been reared in children's homes (run on group cottage lines) because their parents could not cope. Nearly 40 per cent were seen to have a personality disorder, with abnormal interpersonal relations associated with definitely impaired social functioning, compared to just over ten per cent of controls who had never been in care. Nearly 50 per cent possessed a criminal record at, or after, 18, compared to just under 15 per cent of the controls, even given that the control group from inner London contained more socio-pathology than a general population sample. Institutionally-reared women are eight times more likely to become teenage parents (or 40 per cent to five per cent for women in general).

The malign effects are inter-generational. Among women leaving care, pregnancy plays an important part in the processes associated with relationships to unsupportive, deviant men. Starting one's own family partly reflects a tendency to seek escape from an unhappy background and a 'pervasive lack of planning'. But institutional upbringing is strongly associated with parenting, as well as marital, breakdowns. This leads to the offspring going into foster or institutional care for another generation, or at a rate 66 times greater than the children of those who have never needed substitute care. The worst start in life that a child could have is to be born of a young mother who has come out of the care system: 'Nowhere is the cycle of deprivation more obvious than in the admission to care of children whose parents were themselves "in care"'.[81]

As well as the damage to their development which young people in care experience, even when their carers are relatively benign, there is also the added risk of actual physical or sexual abuse. The massive dimensions of abuse over the last few decades are still being revealed, leading to a major review of the 'widespread sexual, physical and emotional abuse of children... over the preceding 20 years',[82] and numerous moves by the Department of Health in the 1990s to get local authorities to bring about changes in management and personnel practice.

It is no longer possible to treat as aberrations cases like that of Frank Beck (a foster carer), who abused dozens of children in Leicestershire between 1973 and 1986, or the Pindown experience, where Tony Latham used a distorted version of Pavlovian conditioning to control children with long periods in isolation. Since 1990 Leicestershire, Staffordshire, Cheshire, Merseyside and North Wales have faced huge police investigations. Peter Howarth, John Allen and Steven Norris, among others, are serving long prison sentences for a sample of their crimes against children in Wales, where a Tribunal of Inquiry was set up in 1996 to investigate events in Clwyd and Gwynedd.[83] At Bryn Estyn in Clwyd, where staff abused boys 'on an almost unimaginable scale',[84] the children also suffered serious physical and sexual assaults at the hands of each other, as staff encouraged peer control to make their job easier.[85] Some of those abused in care themselves become abusers: three from Gwynedd are currently serving life sentences for murder. (The assessment centre in Gwynedd, where so many other abuses took place, closed after its regime collapsed and police were called in to quell disturbances.) Hard on the heels of the scandal in Clwyd—at least 100 children sexually abused over 20 years, of whom ten have killed themselves—came that in Cheshire. By 1997, eleven care workers had been jailed for a multitude of sexual and physical assaults, with more trials pending.[86] In Hackney, Mark Trotter died of AIDS, with many children alleging he had abused them, and when he was due to be charged with abusing children while working in Merseyside.[87]

Up to one in four young women leaving care is either pregnant or already a mother. Sexual intercourse with a girl under 16 is, of course, against the law. Much underage sex is also exploitative. Girls have clearly not been protected from the predatory attentions of either males in the system or outsiders, who may lure or force them into prostitution and live off their earnings.[88] There are allegations too that youths are allowed to work as rent-boys, and to visit the gay scene.[89] A survey by a national drug and alcohol agency found that 44 per cent of its clients had been in care at some time in their childhood. Over a third claimed that they had started using drugs while in institutional or foster care.[90]

The review of residential childcare for the Department of Health in 1991 observed that not only is the 'public parent... not necessarily a successful parent', but that it is misleading to ever couch expectations about public care in terms of the parental role or parental responsibilities.[91] Public care can never 'replace or replicate the selfless character of parental love'. Even 'a warmth and personal concern... goes beyond the traditional expectations of institutions'.[92]

4. WHERE DO WE GO FROM HERE?

We need to bring to an end the present system of treating displaced children in a way which effectively turns them into second-class citizens. The present emphasis on 'family preservation'—i.e. making unlimited attempts to keep children with their biological parent(s), no matter how abusive or neglectful—must be abandoned and replaced with a child welfare system which puts the safety and security of children first.

The grounds on which local authorities can intervene in family life must be narrowly and strictly defined in order to limit the discretion of decision makers. When circumstances require the removal of a child from home, the programme(s) to be used to effect family rehabilitation must be specified, or it must be demonstrated that the parents are unlikely to reform or benefit from services. A deadline—of perhaps 12 months— should be set for the parents to establish their fitness to resume care of their children by, for example, getting off drugs or drink, with case reviews for progress checks. There could be exceptions to 24 months, granted on a case-by-case basis. If parents are unable to comply within the time-span, the process to free the child for adoption should begin.

For children under three and for those involved in serious abuse, a shorter period might apply, and every effort should be made to ensure that children have a safe and settled environment by the age of three. 'Adoption delayed is adoption denied. Although children of all ages can be adopted, children with the best chance of getting and staying adopted are young children.'[93]

Children who have been put into care by their parents voluntarily and then left for over six months should be treated as effectively, if not actually, abandoned. If the child is not freed for adoption at this point, it should only be because of a time-limited plan for the resumption of parental care. There also needs to be a limit to the number of care episodes or other interventions a child can experience, to end the present system under which parents can put their children into care and take them back again as often as they like.

Given the increasing court time taken up by child protection and adoption cases, the 'culture of delay' in family justice has to be tackled. Time limits may have to be built into the legislation to enable adoption proceedings to be expedited, with possible 'fast track' procedures. The aim should be to complete an adoption application in three months, subject to the natural parents' consent. In a genuinely contested case this three-month limit could be extended. This is part of a continuing argument for separating children's cases from the generality of court work, but not necessarily in a separate family court, where it could easily become isolated from the judicial mainstream and simply an arm of the welfare services.[94]

As the freeing system is a lengthy process riddled with delays (and, in many cases, the child is placed before or during the application), it is often suggested that it could be eliminated by making the placing agency party to the adoption application on behalf of would-be adopters. This would provide the forum for dealing with contested cases. However, the chief advantage of freeing is that this takes the worry out of the adoption process for prospective adopters.[95] It was proposed in the 1996 draft adoption bill (which never got to parliament) that placement orders should be available for children who were the subject of care orders, or where parents opposed adoptive placement. These would authorise an agency to place a child for adoption where this was considered to be in the child's best interests.

To dispense with parental consent to an adoption, it now has to be proven that the parents are unreasonably withholding consent, and that it is not possible to rehabilitate the child in the family. Proposals in the 1996 draft bill would have removed legal obstacles to adoption by allowing consent to be dispensed with where the parent cannot be found or is incapable of giving consent (for example, by reason of insanity), or that 'the court is satisfied that the welfare of the child requires consent to be dispensed with', according to a rigorous checklist.

Too often, social services departments have emerged from reports and investigations as extremely inefficient, confused over roles, with a lack of openness and accountability, with inexperienced and unqualified staff at both ground and supervisory levels, and problems about prioritising adoption work.[96] In contrast, it is noted how workers from voluntary agencies are likely to have specialist training in child placement, small caseloads and good supervision.

Being 'seriously worried by the evidence, particularly from local authority social work practitioners',[97] the Review of Adoption Law for the Department of Health and the Law Commission questioned: 'whether local authorities should continue in their present form to have primary responsibility for adoption agency practice'. By 1996 the Social Services Inspectorate also questioned whether the nature and volume of adoption work justified local authorities using an in-house service.[98] There are no good reasons for social services departments to hang on to adoption, when so many are uninterested or even antagonistic, as well as unequipped for the task.[99] It should be handed over to voluntary societies with specialist staffs.

There needs to be a complete separation of adoption work from child protection services. Once an adoption panel has made a recommendation that a child should be freed or placed for adoption, the case should be immediately taken over by agencies specialising in the recruitment and preparation of adoptive families, the placement of children and the provision of professional post-adoption help and support. These agencies, perhaps operating within a franchise system, would be financed by direct grants from central government. So that neither children nor prospective adopters are kept waiting for placements, agencies need to be able to look as widely as they can for suitable adopters, which suggests mutual access to a national pool of available adoptive parents. Agencies which match and prepare the parents and children are probably in the best position to arrange post-adoption services. While it might be preferable for the child to be placed with those of his own racial or ethnic group, this should not delay permanent placement.

These and other measures should take us some way towards realising the aim of a permanent home for every child as the centre of a child welfare system for the twenty-first century. Adoption would not be at the end of the line and no child should have to be written off before reaching it. Instead it would have the priority it deserves as a touchstone of concern for children, and an embodiment of good childcare practice.

Commentaries

Learning from the Past, Planning for the Future

Felicity Collier

PATRICIA Morgan has written a persuasive account of the failings of the British childcare system which she sets graphically against the 'success' of adoption as an option for bringing up children. Her book comes at a time when we understand more than ever before about the inadequacies of the childcare system and the poor outcomes experienced by many children who have been brought up in public care. While strands of her argument are cogent and important, other aspects are confusing, and her conclusion that adoption is the solution to most of these problems is overly simplistic. Morgan's argument that local authorities and social services departments are unable to provide an effective adoption service is also fundamentally flawed.

I want to respond to *Adoption and the Care of Children* by firstly addressing some of my concerns about aspects of the book, in particular: the place and use of adoption; the inherent risk of 'social engineering'; the lessons we must learn from abuses of adoption; and the issue of adoption and 'race'. I will then look briefly at research published by the British Agencies for Adoption and Fostering (BAAF) about the background of children adopted from care in 1996, and conclude by considering what action might increase the use of adoption as an option for looked-after children, other than the radical restructuring suggested by Patricia Morgan.

Adoption: Threat Or Opportunity?

Adoption has, undoubtedly, enabled many children to have stable, happy and permanent families for life. But, while we should celebrate this success, we must not assume that it is the panacea for all of society's problems. We must recognise the risks inherent in any suggestion that adoption is a more successful option for children than returning them to 'lone mothers of low socio-economic status ... likely to have complex and multiple problems'.[1]

Patricia Morgan compares the outcomes for infants relinquished for adoption to a similar cohort of infants reared by their own families. The study quoted[2] concludes that the adopted infants fared better as adolescents than those raised by their birth-families, who comprised 'relatively disadvantaged' young single women. By comparison, the adoptive parents were 'socially advantaged and privileged'. All the children in this study were adopted in 1977 in New Zealand, and we must not forget the enormous societal changes that have occurred between then and now. Adoption in the 1970s was an option taken by many young, single, pregnant women who faced stigma and discrimination within their own families and society, and who often felt that they had no real choice in the matter. They believed that by having their child adopted they were providing them with a better quality of life and removing the stigma of their illegitimacy. The outcomes for children of single pregnant women today in New Zealand and elsewhere will no doubt have improved due to society's acceptance of the children of single mothers and the better support mechanisms now in place.

The suggestion that single mothers ought to be counselled more vigorously about the benefits of adoption today, at a time when there are so many positive single-parent role models, ignores the progress society has made. We cannot—and must not—put the clock back. There was no halcyon age when adoption was the perfect solution. To suggest there was ignores the pain and psychological trauma experienced by so many birth-mothers, some of whom continue to strive to discover whether their child is alive or dead. They have spoken powerfully about their loss and we must listen to them. None of this, of course, negates the successful outcomes for many of the adopted children and the enormous commitment of their adoptive parents, but to imply that it was a pain-free option is clearly not the case.

It is also a sad fact that, for some adopted adults, their early rejection by their birth-mother has left a wound of such proportions on their self-esteem that it has had a negative impact on the rest of their lives. Yes, these children still enjoy the love and commitment of their adoptive families, but at what price? Sue Jardine speaks vividly in her personal testimony:

> Although I do not remember the initial separation from my birth-mother, the experience has had devastating consequences for how I perceive my sense of self and how I have dealt with relationships. As a child I assumed the blame for what had happened to me, and grew up in the belief that I must have been 'bad'–why else would I have been given up for adoption? To be told I was relinquished out of love to give me a better life put me in the position where love is equated with loss. The message that I internalised was that to love would be to take the risk of being rejected again, something I definitely did not want to happen ... As a child, being told I was chosen and special left me wondering why my birth-parents didn't keep me. At a very early age, my security was taken away from me and in my mind there were conflicting messages about why I was born and whether I was wanted.[3]

Family life today is more complex than ever before. Only five per cent of children now grow up in two-parent, two-child families with one parent full-time at home. Many couples have children without marrying, some choose to be single parents; the structure of a family has become much more diverse. This is a fact, not 'political correctness'. If children are well-loved, nourished and cared for within their own families there is thought to be little need for state intervention.

The issue which we must focus on from Morgan's study must not be the decisions taken by young single women but rather the decisions we take in relation to children who are the legal responsibility of the state, children for whom state intervention has been necessary. So, how do we begin to measure successful outcomes for children in care? Patricia Morgan uses a number of indicators such as educational success, stable relationships, secure homes and employment. These are areas where the children of poor and disadvantaged families who do enter care, however briefly, will seldom excel. Morgan acknowledges herself that adoptive parents are a specially selected group of 'ideal' parents offering a great deal to their adopted children, who will clearly benefit from the advantages which their own financial stability and educational attainments bring. It could be said that the cost and effort required to rehabilitate children with their original disadvantaged families will not pay off if outcomes are measured in such terms. However Britain is a signatory to the UN Convention on the Rights of the Child which states that every child should be entitled to live with their original family and that the state should invest resources into making this possible. Indeed, if this were not the case, the wholesale transplanting of children to affluent families could be followed with impunity. To suggest, even obliquely, that there should be less energy and commitment to the safe reunification of families is surely unacceptable.

Many of the children who remain long-term in the childcare system originate from families who continue to care deeply for their absent children. We must not confuse a lack of ability to care with a lack of love. This would be detrimental not only to the birth-families themselves but, more importantly, to their children. Many children in the care system have strong and important links to their birth-parents, siblings and other relatives—the first route to achieving permanence for every child is the safe return to their birth-family or to their extended family. When this is not feasible, even with the proper investment of support, then adoption should be given full consideration, but the lifelong impact of legally severing the link between the child and the birth-family must be given due weight in the decision making. It *is* complex, and to simplify it does everybody an injustice.

The recent inquiry into the circumstances of, and outcomes for, the British child migrants should be a warning to us all. It is shocking to think that, as late as 1969, children were being removed, far too readily, from state institutions to be sent overseas. In many cases birth-families had not contacted their children for only a brief period and yet a decision was made that the children had been abandoned. These confused children arrived in a strange country with no identification documents and thus no way of being reunited with their families in the future. The effects of this migration have affected generations. Indeed, the House of Commons Select Committee reported that:

> ...the dangers of inappropriate adoption are all too real: the evidence we have taken in our current inquiry into the welfare of former British child migrants has shown the emotional damage that can be done when a child is removed unnecessarily from his or her birth-parents.[4]

Patricia Morgan proposes that if, after 12 months, a child in care has not been reunited with his or her birth-family (or attempted reunions have failed) that the child should be placed for adoption. While I strongly reject this proposal for absolute time limits, I do accept that there should be complete clarity at every stage of planning for children in care. This would include holding regular reviews and setting time-scales for both successful reunification of children with their families and for the consideration of adoption as the plan for achieving permanence. Clearly the allocation of appropriate resources to achieve either of these plans would be important. The child's need for permanence and stability must be paramount.

Adoption And 'Race'

Particular attention is given throughout the book to the apparently good outcomes for black children who are trans-racially adopted and the alleged intransigence of social workers who insist on looking for an ethnically matching family. Let us be clear that racism is real and rife in our society and not just a politically correct figment of the liberal consciousness. We need only look to the findings of the McPherson Inquiry into the death of Stephen Lawrence if we require confirmation.[5] This does not negate the success of many trans-racial adoptions, and most social workers would acknowledge that trans-racial adoption is, of course, preferable to a child 'languishing' in an institution.

The reality, however, is that only 3.7 per cent of the total number of children in public care under the age of ten are now placed in residential care. The vast majority will be fostered, often within the extended family under fostering arrangements. It is true that some children in foster care may experience a considerable number of moves, which are clearly detrimental, but a substantial number are only placed with one or two families for the duration of their childhood and will retain a significant attachment to those families. Financial considerations (i.e. loss of a foster-care allowance) mean it is not always possible for foster carers to adopt a child—indeed such considerations will be particularly relevant for less well-off families, and minority ethnic families are disproportionately represented in lower-income groups.

It is important to bear these facts in mind before we too readily move every child in a secure and loving foster family to an adoptive home. Adoption undoubtedly offers a unique opportunity for family life for many children, but other factors must be taken into account. These include, importantly, the children's wishes and feelings, taking into account their age and understanding.

Almost all experts in the field agree, and indeed their views are supported by the Children Act, 1989, that, other things being equal (for example this might exclude cases where there is an existing strong attachment to foster carers), it will be preferable to place a child in a new family which reflects that child's racial, cultural and religious background—this is surely the best way to grow up feeling good about yourself, confident in your identity and able to tackle prejudice and discrimination. It does not mean that other options cannot be successful for individual children and these will need to be explored if necessary to prevent damaging delay, and it does not seek to diminish the commitment of adopters who have adopted children trans-racially with good outcomes. It simply means that, if we know what is the ideal, we should invest resources in trying to achieve it first. Where real efforts are made, it has proved possible to recruit families from the wide range of backgrounds that do reflect the ethnicity of most of the children in multi-ethnic Britain.

Patricia Morgan includes much anecdotal evidence and examples of where 'race' issues allegedly prevented adoption. The experiences related by members of the Association of Trans-racially Adopted People (ATRAP—a support group formed by transracially adopted people who share a common feeling of dislocation) are important for us to hear:

> Few denied they felt loved by their parents and siblings—most realised that love was not enough and that a wide cultural and racial gap had been evident for some time. Many said they felt the difference; however, they were powerless to do anything about it. Although they recognised their feelings of isolation and loneliness, they were unable to express their feelings to their adoptive parents. When they did, they were either ignored or trivialised.[6]

Lynda Ince's study examines the care experiences of a number of black children. The book includes their own powerful testimonies. Listen to Natalie:

> Everyone tends to ask (adults) a lot of questions about why your child is black and you are white. You hear adults asking questions and they know you can hear them. But they tend to ignore you as well because they think that you don't understand. That's mostly my experience.

And Sandra:

> I ended up being racist against black people, 'cause I used to live with white foster people and I think they were racist. They always used to look down on black people.

And Sue:

> Not surprisingly, I was unable to defend myself when racist comments were made about me because I couldn't relate to my Chinese self; I had no strength or pride in having Chinese origins... My physical features betrayed me. Not only did they set me apart from my family but they attracted attention I would rather not have had.[7]

These testimonies are of fundamental importance in countering simplistic statements about trans-racial adoption. Indeed I found it very offensive that Morgan accused social workers of finding black children 'a placement in any black home willing to take them, irrespective of whether this meets their needs'.[8] Patricia Morgan also claimed that the choice of single black adopters for black children in preference to white married couples was also somehow disadvantageous.[9]

I have spoken earlier of the prevalence of single-parent households in our society and the value of single-parent adoption for some children was reiterated again in recent research by Morag Owen. While it is true that one third of Owen's sample of single adopters were black, it is also true that these were remarkably successful adoptions:

> Young black children being placed for cultural reasons could be very rewarding and made excellent progress with single black carers ... There was no indication that boys adopted by single women were progressing badly.[10]

All the adopters in this study had undergone a rigorous assessment process and been approved as suitable adoptive parents. (In fact, Owen suggests that, because of their single status, the assessment process had been much tougher.) They were certainly not a homogenous group or characteristic in any way of multiply disadvantaged single parents; they were confident and mature people who were well supported by friends and members of their extended family. How can it be 'politically correct' (and therefore incorrect) to select single black adopters who will make loving parents and help black and mixed-parentage children feel good and confident about themselves?

Recent Research

In October 1998 BAAF published a research study by Gilles Ivaldi[11] which for the first time analysed key statistical data from the Department of Health database of Looked After Children. It examined the care histories of 1,600 children who were adopted from care in 1996. In many ways, this study confirms Patricia Morgan's concerns; over half of the adopted children entered care when they were less than one year old but the average age at placement for all children in a new family was three-and-a-half years and the average age for adoption was five-and-a-half years.

Undoubtedly, too many children experienced too many delays in care and many had a number of placement moves. But it does also show that most of those children who were adopted had not shuttled between abusive parents and the care system as Morgan suggests: 80 per cent of the children had never returned to their birth-family since first starting to be looked after. However, we cannot afford to be complacent and this study has many implications, such as the need for greater clarity about planning, better information and monitoring about children who remain long term in the care system, and greater efforts required to reduce placement moves and prioritise adoption for children who cannot return to their birth-families.

Future Action To Improve Adoption Services For Children In Care

BAAF has taken the study seriously and we have developed an Action Plan for Improving Adoption Services.[12] I suggest that this is more constructive and has a far greater potential for success than the wholesale removal of responsibility for adoption from local authorities, as Patricia Morgan proposes. Indeed, the connection between good basic childcare practice and local authorities' responsibility for protecting children—including the use of adoption for children who cannot return to their families—is fundamental to social services departments.

It would be totally unproductive to separate adoption from the care of children. In fact it could lead to territorialism as social services departments working with birth-families were expected to refer children on to outside independent or voluntary agencies to arrange adoptions. The short-term effect of any restructuring could only be damaging, and children's lives are too important to allow such posturing. What is needed is a re-injection of resources into local authority adoption services which should not be marginalised. Progress on this is already underway.

In September 1998 the Health Secretary, Frank Dobson, announced new ring-fenced money for children's services under the Quality Protects initiative. Local authorities now need to demonstrate progress on a range of objectives including the maximisation of the use of adoption for looked-after children and the reduction of placement moves. There is an enormous will to make this happen and current evidence is that far more children are being referred more quickly for new families and major reviews of the organisation of local adoption services are underway. For example, 350 children were featured in the February 1999 edition of *Be My Parent* (BAAF's family-finding newspaper) compared to only half that number for the corresponding issue of 1998.

At a time when 'best value' (continuous improvement of services within an efficient, effective and economic framework) is the order of the day, the opportunity for change has never been greater. Many authorities are considering commissioning some aspects of adoption from the voluntary sector or working much more closely together in consortia. It is perhaps true that publications such as *Adoption and the Care of Children* and BAAF's own research, together with the findings of successive child protection inquiries, have helped to prioritise this issue. Now it is important that local authorities have the time to demonstrate that a difference will be made.

BAAF's Action Plan revolves around nine recommendations which, if implemented, would make a significant difference to adoption services. These include the introduction of new comprehensive adoption legislation placing the child's welfare at the paramountcy of all decisions and introducing placement orders in place of the old and time-consuming freeing procedures, which would have a major impact in reducing delay. The introduction and implementation of national standards for adoption services, through a process of consultation similar to that conducted recently in relation to foster care, would introduce greater consistency of practice and could be mandatory on all local authorities and voluntary adoption services.

Introduction of paid adoption leave for adoptive parents would make it much more likely that the range and mix of adopters who can meet the needs of children currently awaiting adoption could be identified. It is a nonsense that even one adoption should be prejudiced because of the inability of an adoptive parent to take on the responsibility of adopting a significantly disadvantaged child because of their inability to take time off paid employment. Thousands of women are entitled to paid maternity leave each year: the argument against extending paid leave to adoptive parents seems to rest on the economic cost to employers. Another measure of financial support which can be given to adoptive parents is the adoption allowance, and I fully concur with Patricia Morgan that the current situation is ridiculous. Children should not be denied the stability that adoption can offer because the loss of a foster-care allowance would financially disadvantage the rest of the family. In effect, this acts as an incentive to retain children in foster care.

The importance of active planning for children in care has already been acknowledged and it is expected that real progress will be made on this issue. The Minister has stated that the introduction of ethnic monitoring of children in care is imminent and this will allow us to speak with confidence about the numbers of black children and children of mixed parentage in care, rather than relying on anecdotal evidence. Patricia Morgan asks important questions about whether black children spend longer in care compared to white children. Ethnic monitoring will help us answer this question.

I agree with Patricia Morgan that local authorities should be required to publish a range of management information about their looked-after child population. Many are indeed now doing so and elected members of social services committees are asking what is happening to the children who are in the long-term care of their authorities. Information about the length of time that children are looked after, consideration of adoption plans, reunification and length of waits for adoption once an adoption plan is made—all these are important.

Perhaps most controversially, BAAF believes that it is important to maintain a national register of all parents who are approved as adopters so that, where a quick placement cannot be made following approval, these families become a national resource for social workers seeking new families. BAAF maintains a computerised database of these families (BAAFLink), but is reliant on local authorities and voluntary adoption agencies referring families to them as early as possible. At the moment there is a mismatch between the numbers of children and the number of families referred to the register. It may be the case that there are simply not enough families to meet the needs of older children, children with disabilities and children who need to be placed with brothers and sisters. All these children make particular demands on prospective adopters. Nevertheless, too many unused approved families contact us at *Be My Parent*. These are often families willing to adopt older children and sibling groups. The opportunity to share these families between local authorities is of vital importance.

The disincentive to share is often a financial one. Local authorities expend considerable resources on the recruitment, support and training of adoptive parents. It is perhaps understandable, but certainly not acceptable, that they are then reluctant to pass these families on and lose potential adoptive parents for their own waiting children. Adopters' lives, however, do not stand still; some go overseas to adopt, others develop new careers and are no longer a resource for children. This is an appalling waste and cannot continue.

Inter-agency fees are also a massive disincentive to the sharing of adopters. When a local authority places a child or children with adopters approved by another authority they must pay a transaction fee. This fee, which can be as much as £15,000, offsets the cost to the voluntary agency or local authority of recruiting and supporting a new family. It is a substantial amount of money for any local authority but a small cost to pay in view of the long-term benefits to society. The price of not paying can be to prejudice the child's opportunity of a secure attachment for life.

Finally, as Patricia Morgan states, post-adoption support is essential. Even if delays through the court system are minimised by new legislation, even if ideal adopters to meet the needs of children are available for every child, even if planning is coherent and achieves permanence within reasonable time scales, there will still be children who have experienced such devastating abuse or neglect at the hands of their birth-families that their long-term development will be affected. We ask adoptive parents to take on a past legacy which will impact on everyone within the family. The least we can do is offer them co-ordinated support which could make the difference between a successful adoption and a disruption. This support will mean social workers being available to offer advice and counselling outside office hours as well as supervising contact arrangements. It will mean co-ordinated educational support and the medical and psychological support for these children that will address the difficulties they face because of their early experiences. Such support does not come cheaply, but our responsibility does not end at adoption and we must recognise this.

Conclusion

It is imperative that all those concerned with the futures of our most vulnerable children now work together to consider how best to facilitate effective adoption where it is indicated. The continuing blaming and castigation of so-called 'politically correct' social workers does nothing to benefit children. We must work together to ensure that prospective adopters understand the background of children currently seeking adoption; that a range of families can be recruited who can meet these children's needs; and that everything is done to minimise delay. We must also strive to reach a common understanding about the appropriate use of adoption in our society and the potential risks of getting it wrong.

A Denial of the Right to Family Life

The Need for Social Services Departments to have More Children Adopted Out Of Care

Jim Richards

Adoption and the Decline of The Family

IT IS little wonder that there is uncertainty and confusion about adoption today, given that the same can be said about the place and content of the family. A brief examination of that institution is needed before consideration is given to the state-sanctioned creation of new families via adoption.

Much of the following is well known. Thus, we have the highest divorce rate in the EU, the longest working hours for fathers and the highest number of births to girls under 16. There has been a social revolution in the care of under-fives, with the creation of what one commentator[1] has described as the mass day-institutionalisation of that age group. This placement of children in daycare occurs earlier and earlier. Whereas in 1979 only 24 per cent of mothers returned to work within nine months of giving birth, this has now increased to 48 per cent, and, ignoring all we know about child development, parents can blithely talk ignorant nonsense about their 12-month-old children being bored at home and ready for social grouping with their peers. In addition, the legal foundation for families, and with it security and rights for children, have suffered massive undermining with the decline in marriage. At the same time, we additionally have the debate about whether or not to enable gay and lesbian couples to 'marry'.

Adoption has to fit into this maelstrom, and it is therefore little wonder perhaps that both this and the previous government have so far lamentably failed to introduce urgently needed new adoption legislation, preferring instead to stay with our existing law, shaped as it was in the seemingly more certain days of the 1960s.

Without a clear political lead, backed by appropriate legislation, those statutory agencies charged with the promotion of adoption—social services departments (SSDs)—are often failing in their tasks. This is in contrast to voluntary adoption agencies, who have been shown to be able to place children with difficult backgrounds more speedily and effectively than their local government colleagues. The voluntary agencies are, though, very much hampered in developing their work because of their reliance on local authorities for referring to them the children who need new families.

Against this background, the following will offer a critical examination of the present government's initiatives, social work attitudes to adoption, and the structure of the statutory agencies charged with the task of finding new families for accommodated children (i.e. those in the care of local authorities) who are unable to return to their birth-parents.

Quality Protects

In September 1998 the Department of Health launched its 'Quality Protects' programme. It aims, by making each local authority submit a Management Action Plan (MAP) annually, to improve steadily both the delivery and outcome of services for children and families. Within it are eight objectives, each with several sub-objectives. One key objective concerns the adoption of children from care.

Objective one aims: 'To ensure that children are securely attached to carers capable of providing safe and effective care for the duration of childhood'. Sub-objectives include the need to reduce the changes of main carers for looked-after children, to increase the use of adoption and to reduce the time it takes to find adoptive homes. However, the indicators by which the above will be tested will not be able to measure the totality of the need for adoption. Thus, all that is asked for is that information is given about the length of time between placing a child for adoption and the granting of the adoption order and the proportion of looked-after children placed for adoption. These are worthwhile indicators, but they are not the central ones. The key ones are: for how many looked-after children is adoption the plan, how many are still awaiting placement and for how long have they been waiting? In addition, authorities should give details of the ages of all other looked-after children and how long they have been in continuous care. This latter information would give some idea of the potential population that may be able to benefit from adoption. Government has chosen to go down the path of managerialism rather than legislation to achieve its policy objectives. However, if this chosen path is to have any chance of success then it is vital that the chosen methods of measurement are both comprehensive and relevant.

Quality Protects brings with it the carrot of extra cash for specified purposes and the stick of not receiving it in subsequent years if targets are not met. It is too early to predict how this mechanism will operate as the first MAPs were only submitted at the end of January 1999. Within adoption though, it is interesting to note that several local authorities have put in bids to the Department of Health for funding for extra adoption workers. This raises two issues. One is that it presupposes that lack of adoption workers is related to the decreasing use of adoption for looked-after children, and the other is that such staff exist in sufficient numbers.

The government, in trying to encourage the greater use of adoption, produced a circular in the autumn of 1998,[2] and this in turn is referred to in the subsequent 'Quality Protects' documentation, outlining, as it does, details of the Department of Health's thoughts on adoption. However, a circular is no substitute for legislation, especially as this one reiterates much that has already been contained in earlier documents from the Department. Indeed a close study of the circular, especially of those areas where it seeks changes and actions, reveals 17 major areas which would be far more effectively handled by legislation. By way of example, these include the need for adoption legislation which enshrines the principal of avoidance of delay, the paramountcy of the child and the monitoring of children's care plans. Exhortation, even with the force of a circular, has failed in the past and will do so in the future unless backed by an act of parliament.

Legislation No Substitute for Skills

Legislation alone, though, is no substitute for skills and experience on the ground, together with those vital ingredients of passionate concern for children and a belief that, for far more children than at present are considered, adoption is a viable option. Social Services Inspectorate (SSI) reports[3] suggest that the first two may often be missing. It has long been a criticism of the present professional training, which leads to the Diploma in Social Work, that it is too short (at two years in length) and its generic base, covering too wide a range of client groups, leaves insufficient time to develop sufficient expertise for child and family work, let alone adoption.

It is not only training that is inadequate to the task, but the present structure of social services departments. Bob Holman[4] in his history of the children's departments and their successor SSDs reminds us of why the former were created. It was in response to a specific tragedy, the murder of Dennis O'Neill by his foster father and the conclusion of Sir James Monckton's inquiry, which was highly critical of the inadequate supervision of the foster home, the use of unqualified staff and a breakdown in communication. The subsequent report by Myra Curtis picked up Sir James' recommendations, in particular that a unified children's department be set up in each local authority headed by a children's officer. Interestingly, it was the expectation that the chief officers should be charged with having 'a personal element' in the exercise of their functions. In other words these officers were not expected to be distant bureaucrats but should be reasonably close to the action. Bob Holman's work gives many examples in which that ideal was more than achieved. He also demonstrates how these focused departments were able to develop high levels of skills and expertise. He does not pretend that all was perfect but in his analysis of the SSDs, set up after the Seebohm report, he charts the decline caused by generically trained social workers, the consequent loss of specialist expertise and the domination of child abuse to the neglect of preventative family work and other skills within childcare.

All this has a negative impact on children. Patricia Morgan,[5] in reviewing the published material, points out what we all know, that there is too much poor practice in the overall care of children by public authorities and that outcomes for children who stay in public care are very poor. Specifically with regard to adoption, despite the attempts by the Department of Health to improve matters, performance at best has been static and at worst in decline (see Table 1, p. 2). She also makes the point that children wait too long, that time scales are insufficiently monitored or managed, (a charge also made by the SSI in a recent report with regards to fostering services[6]), and prior to that the children have too often had too many changes of careers. Meanwhile, the number of looked-after children in England increased (from 49,300 in 1994 to 53,300 in 1998). Those carrying out adoption work are very often inexperienced and so poorly supported that one SSI report spoke of social workers feeling that they were 'left just to flap in the wind'.[7]

Patricia Morgan also comments on SSI reports which revealed evidence that indicates attempts at rehabilitation have been over extended. This is a controversial area, but the SSI language is forthright: 'The consequence of using adoption... as an option of last resort was too great a tolerance for unacceptable parenting behaviour'.[8] This raises a related issue of how adoption is regarded. It should be seen as one of several ways of achieving permanence for children, others being long-term fostering, placement with relatives and, of course, the key one for looked-after children, return to parents. Often, though, adoption is burdened with too many emotional subtexts, which can mean the individual child's needs lose out. There are also indications that adoption is not 'popular' within the profession.

Variations In The Use Of Adoption

Figures have already been quoted for the decline of adoption with regard to children in care. It is worthwhile asking how many children might potentially be available for adoption. As at 31 March 1998, 27,800 children had been in care for more than two years, 20,500 of these had been there for over three years and, of these, 12,100 for more than five years. It is within these figures that the answer lies. The total potentially available for adoption is surely greater than the 2,000 placed in 1998.[9]

There needs also to be comment about the large variations between local authorities in the number of children placed for adoption. For 48 authorities in England in 1996 the figure was less than ten and for several of this group there was a nil return. In 1997 there were 50 authorities placing ten or fewer children. These figures raise questions about the viability of an agency, as well as, possibly, of opposition to adoption. But, in any case, a very low number of children being adopted from one agency is likely to lead to a downward spiral of lack of expertise and lack of focus within a department for seeing adoption as a positive option. It is also worth noting that the number of looked-after children placed for adoption has fallen in recent years despite the increase in the total number of children looked after.

These findings have been further reinforced by the work of Gilles Ivaldi.[10] This research, backed jointly by the British Agencies for Adoption and Fostering (BAAF) and the Department of Health, examined in detail all children adopted from care in 1996. It produced some surprising findings. For instance, the mean age of entry into care of this group of children was surprisingly young, at one year ten months. They also often experienced several movements of foster placement: 48 per cent had two placements, 18 per cent three, and 11 per cent five or more. The mean length of time from entry into care to placement with adopters was one year and nine months. One should never underestimate the difficulty of finding adopters for older children (they tended to wait longer) but the mean figure hides wide variations and it was not unknown for children to have to wait for as long as five years before placement. This is a significant period of any person's life, let alone a child's, and is of particular concern given that the period of waiting was often marred by moves from one foster carer to another, with the inevitable setbacks this can lead to, making the ultimate adoption placement more potentially problematic than might have been the case had it occurred earlier.

Gilles Ivaldi also considered the difference between authorities in the proportion of children adopted out of care. The range was from nil to nine per cent. He went to some lengths to find out why there were such large variations in the use of adoption. He concluded that it was not due to different sociological factors, such as poverty, lone parenthood or unemployment, although these did affect the numbers of children being looked after. Nor did he find that it was related to the level of resources available to adoption workers. This led to his conclusion that different rates of the use of adoption were simply due to the priority attached to adoption and, in stating this, Gilles Ivaldi called for more research into 'the influence of agency culture and value systems on outcomes for children'. It is surely these factors which might largely account for Sutton having 19 per cent of its looked-after children placed for adoption in 1998 whilst six London boroughs placed only one per cent, or for Hartlepool placing 11 per cent and Darlington one per cent.

Ivaldi has called for the improved training of social workers, new legislation and a change in the culture within those authorities whose lack of adoption activity indicates a policy of ignoring, or indeed even being antagonistic towards, adoption. However, the very structure of and growing demands on SSDs may be part of the cause of the low and declining levels of adoption and the delay in finding adopters. These large departments will, in the case of an average-sized unitary authority, spend more than the total expenditure of one of our largest national voluntary childcare agencies, employing several hundred workers across a range of client groups. It is this range which might be at the root of some of the organisational problems. Broadly, in terms of people served, a SSD can be divided into three sections, elderly persons, those adults with psychiatric problems and others with learning difficulties, and children and families. From the point of view of both day-to-day management and elected member involvement, it is a vast span of responsibility with requirements to meet the ever greater expectations of clients and central government and at the same time to organise service delivery in an increasingly demanding environment. One need only consider the care of elderly people to see this. A SSD will need to forge partnerships with hospitals, health authorities, primary care trusts, voluntary and private agencies, as well as manage their own homes and domiciliary services. A similar complex web exists for all client groups. It is true that the Department of Health's circular[11] of 1998 on adoption calls on both directors of SSDs and the social services committees to consider adoption on an annual basis. This is to be welcomed, but the imperative of today can so easily be lost tomorrow, when perhaps more urgent demands move higher up the in-tray. For example, one can sympathise with a director and committee dealing with care in the community of those with a psychiatric illness, especially perhaps in the aftermath of a homicide committed by such a client. Indeed, recent tragic cases have made this area of work a high-profile pressure point.

The Need For Family Departments

Bob Holman's solution,[12] and one with which I wholeheartedly agree, is for family departments to be created. Interestingly, he argues that these new departments should also have responsibility for the youth service and should be overseen by the Department for the Environment, not Health. This is because he sees such a change as being more conducive to creating 'a social environment which allows parents to cope and children to prosper'. With the demise of what he describes as the 'Seebohm Factories', the top managers would be able to develop an exclusive commitment to deprived children and families and have a greater knowledge of individual cases. Moreover, the lines of communication would be both shorter and quicker, enabling decision making to be speedier. This in turn would enhance morale at the coal-face and enable the inspiring leadership of senior managers, which was a feature of the former children's departments, to motivate front line workers.

A recent study of adoption practice has also raised serious concerns about the structural organisation of adoption. In this, Nigel Lowe, Mervyn Murch and others state: 'It is ironic that the children, whose lives are often marred by chaos and unpredictability, are looked after by such large, confusing organisations, almost as if they mirror the children's disordered lives'.[13] This statement is made against their concern about much poor practice which their research revealed. Unlike Bob Holman, they do not advocate a particular solution but they are clear that structural change is of fundamental importance.

If, though, Bob Holman's ideas were put into practice other beneficial changes would occur. Thus the creation of family departments would bring with them family committees where the elected members would equally be able to be more focused on a relatively narrow range of work.

If such a change were brought about, at a national level this would require the creation of a family inspectorate. There would be a greater chance of movement of workers to and fro between departments and inspection, whereas at present it is largely a one-way traffic of middle managers from SSDs to the SSI. Having created these structures, there would inevitably flow a change in training, so that qualifying courses would not be generically based, but one would opt to become someone working with adults or with children and their families. This would be much more akin to the practices in continental Europe and, if the courses were extended to three years instead of two, our qualifications could at last be recognised within the EU.

Other changes within the proposed departments would also flow from the closer links between committees, senior managers and workers. This in turn may lead to more resources being put into the prevention of child abuse on the one hand and adoption on the other. David Thorpe,[14] amongst others, has demonstrated that although there is enormous effort put into detecting child abuse, this is not matched by compensating preventative support being given to families. Moreover, the detection of child abuse has within it strong elements of short-term involvement, whereas preventative work requires, inevitably, a long-term perspective. Likewise, adoption also needs such a perspective. Exhortations from the Department of Health, for social services departments to refocus, do not appear to have led to the necessary changes. Thus, the argument here, is that only by a fundamental restructuring into children and families departments will the necessary redeployment and promotion of long-term family work, including adoption, take place.

Another very important way in which the creation of family departments would lead to better all-round services is that more productive and equal partnerships could be forged with voluntary childcare agencies. This would be particularly so in the field of adoption, where it has been clearly demonstrated that voluntary agencies, once the children are referred by SSDs, are able to place children with difficult histories more quickly, and with greater success, than local authorities, especially because of their superior post-adoption support.

The Need For Change

The continued demise of adoption as a viable option for looked-after children does not flow from one simple cause. Here it is suggested that we need to bring about changes in several areas. Not least the social work profession, as well as many sectors of the wider society, needs to affirm a belief in stable family life as the best basis for the care, love and protection of children. We should also affirm by both belief and research evidence that the combination that works best for children is that of a two-parent family, where mother and father are unified in married love. Mother and father in turn need the backing of society in the form of an at least adequate and predictable income coming from reliable employment. We also need new adoption legislation and a realisation that adoption, as a state-sanctioned process, requires the commitment of government via an act of parliament, which meets the needs of today's children requiring adoption. Central government managerialism, with its targets and promises of cash, will be shown to be insufficient. We also need better trained social workers, operating in a more focused environment–i.e. family departments–better able too work in partnership with voluntary agencies. These changes will be difficult to achieve and the climate is far from promising. However, it must be fought for, otherwise many more children will drift in care, being denied their right to family life, facing the prospect of desperately sad, unfulfilled lives and continuing to fill our prisons and psychiatric hospitals.

Why the Fuss?

The Real and the Symbolic Significance of Trans-racial and Inter-country Adoptions

Barbara Ballis Lal

IN THE early 1970s, trans-racial adoption, itself a reflection of integrationist ideals of the earlier part of the 1960s, was challenged by a relatively small number of social workers in combination with lawyers and ethnic community leaders in the USA.[1] This same course of action occurred slightly later in Britain.[2] Despite being in conflict with the anti-discrimination principle that urges that race/ethnicity be discounted as the basis for determining access to opportunities in education, employment, housing and other valued resources, racial matching initiatives were put forward by those who argued that 'race' or 'ethnicity' was the most important factor in the placement of children available for adoption. Surprisingly, in a political climate in which both diversity and multi-culturalism are increasingly applauded, professionals and other spokespersons insisting upon same race/same ethnicity placements continue to inhibit the formation of families that cross racial and/or ethnic boundaries![3]

The shift from policies and practices that favoured trans-racial and inter-country adoptions to those which prohibited these is

---

Acknowledgements

I would like to thank Nicky Hart and Ivan Light for their incisive comments, so generously given, along with cups of tea, on numerous, early drafts of this essay. Mary Beth Kremmel and Folasade Windokun, always helpful in tracking down articles and statistics, remained patient, cheerful and intellectually stimulating throughout. This research has received ongoing support from The Committee on Research of the Academic Senate of the Los Angeles Division of the University of California.

even more unusual in the light of the available outcome data which demonstrates that, by and large, children in trans-racial/trans-ethnic placements do as well with respect to indicators measuring psychological adjustment and educational achievement as do those children in same-race placements. This body of research is briefly reviewed by Patricia Morgan.[4] When read alongside studies that document the considerable disadvantages of children who remain in foster care (particularly in serial placements) and in both public and private residential institutions, also noted by Morgan, these materials show that adoption, whatever the hues involved, when undertaken with respect to conventional procedures such as home-studies, is preferable to these other options.[5]

Recent government challenges to policies and practices inhibiting trans-racial and trans-national adoptions have proceeded on the grounds of the high costs of keeping children in care, legal considerations, the dubious humanity of preventing children from being placed in permanent family settings, as well as the aforementioned outcome data for adopted, fostered and institutionalised children. In the USA the Multiethnic Placement Act of 1994, amended in 1996 by the Interethnic Adoption Provisions, enacted by the United States Congress, is intended to lessen obstacles to trans-racial and overseas adoptions with respect to agencies receiving federal assistance by deleting race, ethnicity or national origin as criteria determining what are the best interests of the children available for fostering and adoption placements.[6] In Britain, Paul Boateng, when minister, argued that the Children Act, 1989 should be amended in the direction of facilitating rather than excluding trans-racial/ethnic adoption as an acceptable means of placing abandoned and/or abused children in permanent homes.[7] Advocacy groups arguing for unambiguous and simplified regulations facilitating adoptions and lessening the import of racial/ethnic matching policies, alongside of institutionalising clear-cut safeguards for adoptees, are receiving more serious attention in a policy debate previously dominated by professional groups such as the British Agencies for Adoption and Fostering and the Council for the Education and Training of Social Workers which tend to support same-race/ethnic placements.[8] These changes were in keeping with the spirit of the

Hague Convention which states that in those instances in which children cannot be placed in a foster or adoptive home and cared for in their country of origin, inter-country adoption deserves consideration as an alternative way of providing the child with a family.[9]

With respect to actual practice, many social workers and other child welfare experts, including lawyers, resist both making trans-racial placements and approving inter-country adoption petitions despite outcome data, changes to existing legislation and the sentiments of many voluntary associations. The reluctance of these professionals is supported by a variety of community leaders, the personal testimonies of some adult trans-racial adoptees and a relatively small number of studies which either conclude that trans-racial and inter-country adoptions are altogether harmful or which outline some of the alleged risks of these types of adoption not characteristic of same-race placements.[10]

The defence of same-race placements despite the thrust of available outcome evidence, and the resistance to changes in legislation contesting this discriminatory policy principle, are a reflection of the critical issues, real and symbolic, underlying debate about trans-racial and inter-country adoption. These issues have to do with first, what constitutes a desirable family and what counts as appropriate parenting. Thus, for example, Morgan and others have pointed out the consequences, mostly undesirable, of the currently fashionable belief that family preservation is always in the best interests of the child. As a result biological mothers who might previously have decided or been advised to give up their babies for adoption on the grounds of young age and interruption of schooling, being unmarried and without a steady partner, being unemployed and without financial assets, are now encouraged to keep their babies regardless of the harm this might result in for both mother and child. 'Biologism' and 'the "privileged position" of biological kinship' undermines the claim that both mothering and family life have social and moral dimensions based upon commitment, care and the nurturing of children in a secure and stable environment over a lifetime which can exist either alongside or in the absence of biological ties.[11]

A second issue concerns the prospects for the incorporation of people of colour into predominantly white societies which are perceived as being both racist and class-ridden. However reluctantly, opponents of trans-racial and inter-country adoptions cast non-white adoptees as foot-soldiers in an effort to obtain racial justice and social equality. A perception of the failure of the Civil Rights Movement in the USA to alter life chances for non-whites and the persistence of a range of discriminatory behaviour, despite the important changes in federal legislation during the 1950s and 1960s, has driven many intellectuals and others in positions of leadership, to consider integration and assimilation as unobtainable and undesirable.[12]

Of greatest import to the debate about trans-racial and inter-country adoption, however, are issues stemming from the discovery of 'identity' by academics, professionals, politicians and community leaders, and, in particular, those 'collective identities' organised around race, ethnicity, gender and sexual orientation.[13]

Identity, Politics and Therapy

The arguments of advocates of same-race placements are based upon 'identity essentialism' and their objections to trans-racial/ethnic placements construct 'identity deficits'.[14] An 'essentialist' model of identity argues that one facet of a person, such as race, ethnicity, gender or sexual orientation, 'trumps' all other conceptions of selfhood, including those based upon a combination of identities representing a variety of social bonds and affiliations of varying degrees of both generality and intensity.

Identity essentialism is rooted in the 'politics of identity' and the perspectives of black power and feminism which captured the imaginations of academics, professionals, and a variety of political constituencies in the late 1960s. Identity politics continues to be of scholarly as well as of more general interest and remains an important basis for political organisation and the mobilisation of new social movements undermining the privileged position once occupied by the politics of social class.[15] The appeal of the politics of identity as a political strategy has always been enhanced by presumed therapeutic properties attendant on identity seeking and identity affirmation. Consciousness-raising leading to individual liberation and collective empowerment are the promised results of reorganising a sense of self around a suppressed and marginalised essentialist identity.[16]

In assuming that one feature of the person such as race or ethnicity determines experience and life chances, and ties individual destiny to that of the group, identity essentialism overlooks variations among members of a putative group. For example, ethnic identity essentialism overlooks the importance of social class and generation in effecting differences between African-Americans[17] and non-white Britains.[18] Reversely, the effects of the mass media and of consumerism in contributing to similarities in aspirations and lifestyle between ethnic minorities and a dominant white group, especially with respect to generational cohorts of adolescents and young adults, is overlooked .[19]

With respect to children in care, identity essentialism emphasises the benefits of knowing who you are as a consequence of either biological descent or 'socially constructed' attributes such as 'race', and of participation in collectivities organised around an essentialist identity. These benefits are thought to exceed the advantages of being fed, clothed, housed, schooled, and emotionally supported by adoptive parents and siblings representing a different race or ethnic group. Where biological parents, and especially mothers, are absent or incapacitated, their children are presumed to 'belong' to their community of birth.

Thus, in an oft-quoted statement issued in 1978, the National Association of Black Social Workers (NABSW) in the USA argued that:

> Black children belong physically, psychologically, and culturally in black families in order that they receive the total sense of themselves and develop a sound projection of their future... Black children must not lose their cultural identity by being reared in a white home... It is imperative that black children learn that there are cultural differences between black and white and that black culture provides a viable positive way of life.[20]

The NABSW continues to argue that:

> Trans-racial adoption of an African-American child should only be considered after documented evidence of unsuccessful same-race placements has been reviewed and supported by appropriate representatives of the African-American community.[21]

In a recent statement the National Association of Social Workers agrees that: 'An effort to maintain a child's identity and her or his ethnic heritage should prevail in all services and placement actions that involve children in foster care and adoption programs'.[22]

In a similar vein, a 'practice note' issued by British Agencies for Adoption and Fostering (BAAF) directs that 'the placement of choice for a black child is always a black family' in which socialisation to the requirements of a black identity and a black culture would be assured. Moreover, the note continues, under many circumstances leaving children in 'residential placement in a unit with appropriately trained and experienced staff' is preferred to trans-racial placement.[23] More recently, a BAAF circular on inter-country adoption advises prospective adopters of their intention to follow the practices regulating adoption within the UK, which gives precedence to placing children in care with a 'family of the same heritage' as mandated in the Children Act, 1989 in England and Wales and the Children (Scotland) Act of 1995. This circular notes 'the difficulties children can face when establishing their identity and when trying to cope with prejudice and racism while growing up in British society'. The authors go on to observe that children who look different from their adoptive parents and 'have continually to explain their adoptive status' to others 'may feel very confused and angry about their identity'. They conclude that: 'Any adopted child feels some confusion of identity and being trans-racially adopted can compound this confusion'.[24]

In the above and other policy statements by child welfare professionals, as well as in research, newspaper and magazine articles, radio and television shows, and in testimonies to government committees, advocates of same-race placements express their concerns about the outcome of trans-racial and inter-country adoptions with respect to a range of identity deficits. These deficits include confusion about who one is and where one 'belongs', anger, low self-esteem, self-hatred, inability to deal with racism, alienation, lack of knowledge of roots and culture of descent and an inability to make friends, all of which may or may not be expressed as emotional instability, lack of achievement in school and career, flight from adoptive parents, search for biological roots, delinquency and deviance.[25] As already pointed out, these gloomy prognostications are not borne out by the outcome data to hand.

Identity deficits attendant on trans-racial domestic adoptions are sometimes thought to be exacerbated with respect to inter-country adoptions, even if children 'appear more similar in colour and aspects of culture' to their adoptive parents. Thus, the 1998 BAAF information and guidance circular, already referred to above, points out with regard to inter-country adoptees:

> Not only are they potentially isolated within the family, they're likely to be isolated within the country too. For a child of a different ethnicity adopted from overseas, it may be that he or she has lost touch with many aspects of their culture, such as language, religion, diet, customs, etc. So later difficulties around knowing 'who they are' can result in a feeling of alienation from their community of origin. Even if a child has not had direct experience of their culture i.e. if he or she has been adopted as a very young baby, the importance of a sense of roots must never be underestimated.

The authors conclude:

> Culture is a powerful motivating force for adopted people. A child's right to knowledge about their heritage should not be underplayed or undervalued. Placing a child with a family which shares his/her heritage will give the child a better chance of developing a positive sense of themselves and healthy self-esteem.[26]

In addition to reiterating a concern with regard to the identity deficits already noted, in this statement BAAF makes the fatal error of supposing that culture is inherited so that an infant adopted at an early age is in some primordial way attached to a community and culture of biological descent, whose significance is at least as important as the community and culture within which it has been nurtured and grown up.

Second, while the benefits of knowing about 'language, religion, diet, and customs' are acknowledged, nothing is said about the way in which cultures and heritages may see illegitimacy, being female, being orphaned, infirmity or birth defect, poverty and any number of other factors which would condemn overseas adoptees to precarious and miserable lives in their countries of origin. For example, consider the prospects for survival of 'street children' in many South American countries, such as Brazil, particularly as a result of unofficial government policies to rid their cities of such children.[27] Knowledge about preferences for male children as an expression of religious practice in India and China and the prospects for abandoned female babies are certainly as central to culture and heritage as diet.[28]

Third, cultures are not fixed. What constitutes a culture or a heritage is subject to changes in environment, for example, those changes brought about by globalisation including the movement of goods, people, and access to the mass media which blur the distinctions between ethnic groups and with respect to inter-country adoption, between sending and receiving societies. Moreover, what is believed to be salient with regard to culture and heritages also changes in an ongoing flux of interpretations, re-interpretations and 'inventions' of political, intellectual, professional, media and consumer leadership.

An alternative to essentialism is a perspective which insists that identity is oriented to affiliations based upon consent, such as occupation and political party, as well as social bonds based upon descent.[29] The labile and contextual approach to identity, as opposed to the essentialist model, argues that individuals and groups see themselves with respect to others in many different ways. Self-conception is a creative process, both changeable and self-interested although subject to constraints, such as the understandings and behaviour of others in particular situations and conventions and norms. Generation and age-cohort are particularly potent sources of identity. In democratic, open societies, individuals can exercise varying degrees of choice with respect to self-conception.[30]

A labile and contextual perspective on identity as opposed to an essentialist point of view suggests that children adopted trans-racially and inter-ethnically can be expected to create a functional and adaptive sense of self, as do other children in a variety of non-conventional family settings. These children may be expected to undertake 'identity work' not unlike that required by children in mixed-race/mixed-ethnicity biological families,[31] or one-and one-half and second generation non-white children of immigrants.[32]

Adopted children have issues to resolve with respect to their adoptive status that are additional to the tasks of negotiating who they are and where they belong faced by children who live with biological parents.[33] Coming to terms with having been rejected or given up for adoption by birth-parents is one such painful task. A second task, shared with children in mixed-race/mixed ethnicity biological families, concerns questions by others, such as peers and teachers, about the physical differences between an adoptee and one or both adoptive parents and possibly siblings. However, the solution to the difficulties raised by the questions of others is not to discourage trans-racial/trans-ethnic families, whether adoptive or biological. Rather, the solution lies in educating extended family members, neighbours and friends as well as teachers, child welfare professionals and other persons in authoritative positions to treat racially and ethnically diverse families, whether adoptive or biological, as an acceptable and valued form of family life.

Child welfare workers, as well as adoptive parents, might wish to do away with the additional hurdles that trans-racial/trans-ethnically adopted children confront. However, as Patricia Morgan concludes, whatever the difficulties presented by adoption, including trans-racial/trans-ethnic adoption, it is likely that the resources provided by a stable family will far exceed those available in foster and residential settings, thus enabling children to cope with all manner of challenges that their environment presents to them, including racism.

Identity Essentialism and Ethnic Identity Entrepreneurs

To the child welfare 'ethnic identity entrepreneur'[34] falls the task of designing programmes and policies for children in care that do not result in identity deficits.

Three attributes characterise ethnic identity entrepreneurs. First, ethnic identity entrepreneurs appeal to an essentialized image of identity. In some instances, such an appeal is to an already existing and institutionalised representation. For example, in the 1960s black power advocates did not have to create or discover colour as an essential feature of being African -American. Rather, the significance of colour was the outcome of designations of white Americans, and already institutionalised in history, law, convention and culture.[35]

Second, ethnic identity entrepreneurs invoke this essentialised identity and group membership to justify a claim to, or monopolisation of, scarce resources, such as jobs or professional advancement and entitlements, by way of a process of social closure.[36] Not all child welfare professionals are ethnic entrepreneurs (and not all ethnic identity entrepreneurs are child welfare professionals). The emergence of ethnic identity entrepreneurs depends upon incentives and opportunities to develop strategies of social closure.

Third, the activities of ethnic identity entrepreneurs which are often initially motivated by the desire to open up options and to facilitate choice among members, instead induces conformity and functions as a mechanism of social control. Child welfare advocates of same-race adoptions who work in bureaucracies—whether governmental or community-based—acquire a very extensive power by virtue of their office and their professional expertise which enables them to construct and enforce their specific conceptions of what ethnic identity is and the cultural requirements this essentialised identity entails. They are gatekeepers in the 'institutional processing of the self' and are among those 'well-placed persons who are in a position to give official imprint to versions of reality'.[37]

Conclusion

Discrediting trans-racial and inter-country adoptions has more to do with a prevailing climate of politically motivated opinion and professional advantage than would be warranted on either the basis of outcome data on trans-racial and inter-country adoptees or research findings evaluating fostering and institutional care as alternatives to adoption.

Ultimately, the real significance of obstacles to adoption across racial, ethnic or national boundaries is measured by the number of children who remain in foster or institutional care, or with biological parents unable or unwilling to look after them. It is difficult to estimate the number of children who experience this miserable and damaging fate. However, even one such case represents a failure on the part of adults to act decisively in 'the best interest of the child'.[38]

What Next for the Children?
A Blueprint for Reforming Child Welfare

Conna Craig

BOTH the UK and the USA are failing the most disadvantaged segment of modern Western society. Patricia Morgan painstakingly delineates that failure—from the abandoned child who because of unfiled paperwork waits years for an adoptive family, to the systematic sexual predation on children in state-run foster homes and institutions. Children in foster care—indeed all children—deserve better.

Where Do We Go From Here?

There exists enough rigorous and longitudinal research for the policy maker and the general public to reach a verdict: the system (in each country) of public agency child welfare needs not just repair, but overhaul.

Radical reform is in order. Accountability must be the principal component of the re-shaped system. Families of origin—that is, the biological families—must be held accountable for their behaviour and be given a strict timeline—one year—to prove fitness to resume care of their children. Foster carers should be accountable for the safety of the children in their homes, and for the manner in which the carers spend foster-care stipends. Local authorities should no longer be allowed to hide behind a veil of confidentiality or plead the excuses of children having 'special needs' or being too 'hard to place' for adoption. At the end of this chapter is a list of specific reforms. None is earth-shattering. Some of the recommendations could be put to work for the children immediately (an example is the removal of barriers to trans-racial adoption). Some but not all of the blueprint recommendations would require capital investment. A simple linear equation of current system expenditures, plus ancillary costs relating to the system's failure to place children in permanent adoptive homes, would set a point at which a financial return could be expected. The return, in human value, is immeasurable.

Child welfare reform is not rocket science. True reform is rooted in basic social and economic principles. The process begins as the state intervenes when abuse or neglect occurs. When the state gains custody of the child, the goals must be clear, measurable and achieved in a timely manner, with the emphasis on child–not parental–well-being. Children need safety, physical and emotional nourishment, stability, care for their health and educational needs, and one thing the state can never be: a loving, permanent family.

Ideologies run deep and have become entrenched. Most troubling is the belief that only the public sector can adequately care for the parentless child. Also problematic is the notion that trans-racial adoption is damaging to children and to entire minority cultures. Furthermore, though this has been consistently disproved, there is a sense that the status of adoption is more burdensome than a loveless childhood. The obstacles to change are not only the complexity of regulation and funding streams, but also ideological opposition to a new, more efficient, more humane approach to helping children.

Some will argue that the goal of today's national programmes is to keep the family together. However, re-abuse rates of foster children who were returned from care to their families of origin demonstrate that some biological groupings are not families in the traditional, natural sense: a set of related individuals, the strongest of whom protects the others. Take a look at the abused two-year-old returned by a local authority to a crack-addicted mother and jailed father, for the sake of family preservation or cultural continuity. Is this a family? What is being preserved, it appears, is something else entirely. State programmes and related funding schemes are perpetuated. Bureaucrats' job security is practically guaranteed.

In the quest to re-unite children with their biological families, a false idea is maintained: if only the right mix of government funding and state involvement were concocted, it would prevent parents from abusing and re-abusing their children. This type of thinking has led to unconscionable decisions. In two US cases during the same week in the same state, a judge 'freed adults who admitted repeatedly beating or raping a child in their care'.[1] The judge claimed that a 43-year-old man who began raping his wife's daughter when the girl was 11 was not a predator, but 'acted out in response to stress in the family'. The judge reasoned that jailing the rapist would create financial hardship for the family. The same judge sent a mother of three, a woman who had savagely beaten her daughter with belts and electrical cords, not to jail but to anger management classes.

Change of Heart

First, the very idea of 'unadoptability' would have to be reasoned out in order to meaningfully restructure the system. Every child is adoptable. The data show the success of adoption of all types of children. One need only look at the results of finalised adoptions in the US and UK. Furthermore, there are waiting lists for children of all ages and types and ethnic backgrounds. This includes children with AIDS, teens, even children who must remain hospitalised for chronic physical or mental conditions yet still benefit from the security of belonging to a permanent family.

Next, the 'adoption stigma' excuse is without merit. Adoption's bad name does not hold up against evidence. For centuries adoption has been recognised as a caring alternative to allowing a child to remain in danger. Findings on well-adjusted adopted children and adoptive families to which Morgan refers should, at least in a policy forum, combat the discrediting of adoption.

Tragically, in practice–in both the UK and the US–adoption today is not considered a gift of loving generosity, but a last resort. Here is the third fundamental change that must take place: recognition that adoption is a valid means by which to build a family. That basic tenet must be accepted before the debate on reform can become meaningful. Policy makers, academics and practitioners who do not believe in adoption are not going to build or carry out adoption policy that works for children or for society. This is especially relevant in trans-racial adoption policy and practice, where three decades of research findings can no longer be ignored by race-obsessed judges, social workers and commentators.

Morgan discusses the status of adoption but only briefly (referring to Bowlby) mentions the trauma of initial loss.[2] It is not being adopted that is painful; it is that somewhere, someone on whom the child should have been able to depend was unwilling or unable or unavailable to care for that child. If an argument against adoption is that given-up or taken-away children are already doomed, then we have lost some sense of humanity. Current child welfare practices put adoption low on the family services continuum, overlooking that it is not adoption, *per se*, that causes pain, but what has occurred before that. The initial loss is a tragic one. However, like many other losses, it is not terminal. We owe every one of these children the chance to grow up in a permanent, loving family.

In instances of abuse and neglect, rather than stopping the infliction of pain on a child, today's policies call first for sending the child back into the fire. Adoption, it is argued, is too painful for children who have already been badly hurt. The synchronal argument is that hurt children are so 'damaged' that they cannot function in a family, therefore adoption is not to be considered.

Pigeons and the Crumbs

Let us admit that—as current policies and practices stand—we are throwing away part of a generation of children who have committed no crime. These children have asked for nothing; for the vast majority, the reason for being in state care is that a crime has been committed against them. Now the state perpetuates child abuse and neglect and paedophilia as it (a) returns children to known offenders; (b) places children in foul and dangerous foster homes; and (c) prevents the children who are legally free for adoption from enjoying the freedom to be kept safe and loved.

The current system lays the groundwork for criminality, homelessness and unwed pregnancy. As Morgan and others have attested, foster-care children are highly over-represented among populations of prison inmates, runaways, and teen mothers.[3]

Critics of adoption are quick to point out that adopted children have been found to utilise mental health services at a slightly higher rate than the general population. This higher rate of use could be attributed to adoptive parental awareness of the children's need to talk through their initial loss. At any rate, seeking professional counselling is not a character indictment, and is not related to pathological behaviour.

Adoption is not a fairy tale. It is a viable means of forming a permanent family in which the government plays no more extensive role than it would in a biological or step-family. The finalisation of adoption does not erase early loss. It does something else: it recognises and treats that loss, and offers the child the permanency of new familial bonds, something that no state agency has to offer.

The alternative? Every week in America a conference is offered on some new way to approach the foster-care 'crisis'. We hear of parenting from prison; placing infants with their biological mothers in drug rehabilitation houses; kinship care with relatives so distant (yet of the same skin colour) that the child has never before met them; and the re-instatement of the orphanage. None of the above has a track record of promoting the well-being of children. Each reinforces the obvious: no government has ever developed any programme that can equal a family.

Adoption—including older adoption, trans-racial adoption, the adoption of handicapped children, and sibling adoption—promotes the well-being of children. It appears that only ideological arguments, racism and long-term investment in maintaining the status quo will stand in the way of our most vulnerable children growing up in permanent, loving families.

Blueprint: Recommendations for Policy Reform

- Stop the equalisation in policy and practice of adoption and other forms of long-term care. As Morgan has demonstrated, the outcomes for adopted children are far more positive by a variety of critical measurements than are outcomes for children who reach the age of majority in the foster-care system.
- The framework for adoption policies must be based on the

rights of children, not the ideology of policy makers or social-work professionals. Therefore, no child shall be labelled 'unadoptable' by any public or private organisation.

- Trans-racial adoption must be given full legal sanction.
- The national government must immediately require local authorities to (a) report on outcomes of care given and status of children currently in care; (b) give a full accounting of costs; (c) develop outcome measurements and issue requests for proposals from private, charitable and faith-based organisations without regard to geography.
- A timeline of 12 months, with a one-time exception to 24 months, must be placed on the family of origin to demonstrate its capacity to care for children who have been removed due to abuse or neglect, or who have been voluntarily placed in care.
- Once a child is legally free for adoption, local authorities must make this known to private agencies without regard to geography.
- Foster and adoptive parents must be licensed to a higher standard than currently exists. Along with recently-required criminal records checks, there must be yearly re-licensing procedures. As a starting-point model, the UK could look to Massachusetts, which in late 1998 became 'one of the few states to require that foster parents be literate, have adequate income, and get yearly training'.[4] Limits should be placed on the number of children each foster carer—those who are already licensed as well as new licensees—can look after at any one time.

The development of an approach which promotes adoption without delay would ultimately save many children. The responsibility for financial and emotional care would rest on the adoptive parents rather than local authorities. Huge amounts of funds would no longer be wasted on perpetuating a broken system. Most important, such an approach will give thousands of children the chance for a better future.

A Fringe Element of Social Policies?

Radical Proposals for the Reform of the Public Childcare System

Chris Hanvey

THE UK childcare establishment has become a major threat to the welfare of children.

The contracting—in both senses of the word—of the welfare state, the professional rivalries and turf wars between health, education and social services and a public lack of confidence in existing organisations have conspired to create what can only be regarded as a crisis in public childcare. If, as the Chancellor, Gordon Brown, announced, his welfare-to-work programme, cash injections, assisted pre-school and nursery proposals mark 'the first step to a childcare strategy for the United Kingdom',[1] in which childcare will no longer be a 'fringe element', then there is still a long way to go.

Now, 'crisis' is a vastly over-rated word and should only be used very sparingly. Where is the evidence that the present situation has become intolerable? Is Patricia Morgan's work on adoption, for example, with its evidence of ideological and practical muddle,[2] just one example of a system that otherwise serves children well? Below is a selection of many possible examples which help to illustrate the point that crisis is not too strong a word to use.

In 1974 the *Report of the Committee of Inquiry into the Care and Supervision Provided in Relation to Maria Colwell*[3] was published. It recounted the events which had led to Maria's death, at the hands of her step-father, William Kepple. It was to prove a defining moment, not only in the development of childcare, but in the wider history of welfare provision in the UK. Only three years previously, local authority social services departments had been established in England and Wales, following the recommendations of the Seebohm Committee Report, which aimed to create one door through which all social problems would enter. Instead of a family receiving the services of a welfare officer, a childcare officer, a mental welfare officer and, if they were particularly unlucky, a probation officer as well, they would be assisted by an all-singing, all-dancing generic social worker who would provide a comprehensive service to the whole family. It heralded a brave new world and was, like the establishment of the NHS, based on the unspoken assumption that a finite number of social problems would eventually be absorbed by the new Seebohm social services departments. Then, three years later, with all the frailty that human systems are heir to, it was found to be fallible, with the death of a neglected child. Ironically, it had been the death of a child that had led to the last major childcare re-organisation and the establishment of Children's Departments, after the reforming 1948 Children Act.

The Maria Colwell inquiry was to become a watershed and the subsequent years have seen a sad roll-call of children killed at the hands of family or 'carers', where the co-ordinated services of health, education, police and social services have often been lacking. The reports into the deaths of, for example, Jasmine Beckford (London Borough of Brent,1985), Kimberley Carlile (London Borough of Greenwich,1987), Tyra Henry (London Borough of Lambeth,1987) and the Cleveland Inquiry (1987) have done much to drive a nail into the coffin of public confidence. More recently, in 1999, the media interest in a couple of foster carers living a nomadic existence, in order to maintain their relationship with two children, points to a wide discrepancy between public and professional perceptions of childcare. The state continually demonstrates, as Patricia Morgan asserts in another context, that it often makes a very bad parent.[4]

Area Child Protection Committees (ACPC's), established at a local level to co-ordinate services for vulnerable children, have largely failed, because of professional boundaries and an unwillingness to share resources. Made up of the major statutory players in children's lives—social services, health, education, probation, NSPCC and the police—they have no remit to pool or divide resources for the good of children and, in some areas, find it difficult enough to contribute very small amounts towards the shared training of professional staff. They are powerless to affect the near breakdown in some local authority social services departments, where child protection cases can remain unallocated and only the most urgent crisis situations receive attention. Only—and it is the central tenet of this chapter—when resources are shared will there be any real chance of improved, co-ordinated services.

But a counter-argument might be that this is just one, isolated example of failing children's services. Unfortunately this is not the case. For instance, it is little more that a cliché to assert that the most damaged children in the whole of the UK childcare system, who end up in children's and adolescent homes, are looked after by the most ill-qualified staff. Indeed, the majority of such staff have no formal qualifications or training. Yet, they are expected to deal with children and young people who, having been removed from their own 'carers' because of abuse or neglect, have frequently experienced multiple placements in foster homes, before an eventual removal to institutional care. A recent investigation by Barnardos[5] revealed that many such children have been moved numerous times, each move contributing to and, on many occasions creating, more damage than the original reasons for placement in public care. The case of Frank Beck, the North Wales inquiry, chaired by Sir Ronald Waterhouse, recent investigations in Cheshire and Sir William Utting's report *People Like Us*, testify to a public care system which, in Sir William's words provides 'a crash course in human (predominantly male) wickedness'.[6]

The consequence for local children's homes (which have become powder kegs of instability and the focus for local complaint or adverse publicity) has been a gradual withdrawal, by local authorities, and to some extent voluntary organisations, from providing children's residential care. This is the result of a number of other equally complex factors: the wish of the last conservative governments under Margaret Thatcher and John Major to encourage a mixed economy of care, a desire by local authorities to abandon costly and often scandal-ridden establishments for some of the most troubled and troublesome young people and, to some extent, the growth of the private sector running residential care as the voluntary sector withdraws. In human terms this results in some children who have, even by the young age of ten, experienced multiple placements and yet more social workers.

This raises a fundamental issue which both prompts comparisons with America and is at the heart of current UK childcare difficulties: the disintegration of any coherent overall strategy. While the 'mixed economy of care' might provide a useful model for adult services—where choice is desirable—it can lead to fractured, unco-ordinated children's services. Two examples may help to demonstrate this point.

There is strong evidence for the view that the American system—where the rump of statutory services (mainly child protection and juvenile justice) is provided by the state, with everything else supplied by a mixture of 'not-for-profit' bodies and the private sector—is creeping upon the UK by default. As local authorities pull back from running services, childcare provision has become an increasingly broad church, with private homes, some private fostering services, voluntary adoption agencies and innovative but often isolated community-based projects, such as family centres, run by voluntary organisations. There is no consistency across various areas of the country as to what public services for children may be available: each region or district has a history of *ad hoc* developments that, like Topsy, just 'growed'. And, amidst all this confusion, remain local authority social services departments. They are battling to retain the semblance of children's provision yet are reduced to a crisis service for abused children while, at the same time, they must implement community care policies for adults.

One more example of this lack of co-ordination suffices. It extends beyond the social welfare organisations to other disciplines such as medicine and education where children's services are also, equally, vital. Sometimes, for example, it becomes necessary to obtain special provision for a child, which results in the need for a distant residential resource. (In extreme cases, such resources can incur annual costs of over £150,000 a year.) The consequence, once such placements have been found, is often a fiercely fought debate as to whether the child's predominant needs are social, educational or medical. A successful outcome, so far as the representatives of each department are concerned, will result in another department picking up the bill. Sometimes such battles are just not resolved or are fudged to such an extent that the child's needs remain unmet. 'Is it a medical, or is it a social problem?' seems a sterile way of ensuring that the best interests of an individual child are met.

The result is that children's services are, by default, fast deteriorating. It is not through malice or incompetence, but through a combination of vested interest, segregated responsibilities and a lack of any central co-ordination. Significantly, perhaps, children's services did not receive the kind of 1997 election coverage that education did (although education is clearly one vital area of children's services), nor did children's needs figure in any of the major parties' manifestos. Instead we find ourselves superficially bounced by the media. On the one hand there is despair at the grainy images of the two children who killed James Bulger and outrage when child abuse tragedies hit the press. On the other hand there is a confusing sentimentality regarding foster carers who take children away and an almost total cynicism at reported cases of responsible adults abusing those in their care.

It is within this context, too, that Patricia Morgan's views need to be seen. Arguing for a more central role for adoption, she makes two powerful points.[7] The first is that adoption should be seen, much earlier, as the best option for children, offering stability, permanence and a childhood free from welfare interference. Second, that for this to happen, there may need to be a new agency that deals with adoption, led by skilled practitioners who focus exclusively on this area of work. While this may seem persuasive, it ignores the wider context within which adoption is organised and of which it is a part of any comprehensive childcare strategy. The solution for sound childcare services has to be even more radical and is outlined below.

But why not leave children's services to evolve, rather than impose yet more structural change? After all, they are vast consumers of the public purse. In 1995-96, £700 million was spent on child abuse services alone and the 40,000 children on the non-accidental injury registers cost £1,083 million.[8] Any changes to current structures are, furthermore, likely to incur further costs. If we were to adopt this kind of wait-and-see approach, the following consequences are likely to ensue. First, regardless of government, local authority services will contract. Local authorities are increasingly becoming the commissioners, rather than providers of services, with voluntary, rather than private sector organisations, becoming the preferred partners. The consequence of this is that voluntary organisations will become even larger suppliers of services that were previously seen as state responsibilities, albeit that these services may be patchy and subject to huge regional or local variations. At the same time, and as a second consequence, we are likely to see a steady growth of small, lottery-funded childcare projects which in their brief life from chrysalis to butterfly grow, flourish and then die. The inevitable questions this all raises are, firstly, whether a growing and largely unaccountable voluntary sector is any better than present arrangements? And secondly, whether children's interests are best served by a situation in which a thousand flowers bloom, but an holistic approach to children's needs remains sadly lacking?

The third consequence of no action will be some inevitable growth in private sector provision for children. Sometimes, this will be offered by former disillusioned providers of local authority services, such as foster carers, who are no longer prepared to tolerate the current low levels of local authority support. Sometimes, these private provisions will be for commercial reasons, such as the proposals for private secure accommodation where a good return on shareholder capital is the main incentive. No matter which side of the political divide one sits on over this issue, it remains certain that it will contribute to the bifurcation of childcare services and make much more difficult a co-ordinated approach to public childcare.

We are also likely to see an increased dissonance between social services and education, as a result of implemented and proposed educational reform. Increasingly, schools are not able to provide for those educational failures who, sadly, make up the majority of the public childcare system and let down the school league tables. Social support to schools is often seen as a costly extra that few educational establishments can afford. And so, at a time when the two services should be moving closer (since schools provide invaluable indicators of family 'dis-ease'), they are moving further apart.

Finally, given current pressures on health authorities, the acute care funding crisis and the inability to provide comprehensive child mental health services, for example, there is likely to be little progress towards integrated health and welfare services. All of this points towards a nightmare scenario of not-for-profit organisations operating with no co-ordination, no incentives for working together, and hard-pressed statutory social services only able to deal with crisis child protection work.

Where then, if we are to address this institutional decline in our public childcare services, does the future lie? Should there be a social welfare equivalent of Ofsted (perhaps OfCare?) which would attempt to impose common standards on the huge diversity of UK childcare provision? The difficulty with this kind of approach is that childcare provision is much more diffuse than the education sector. It would be difficult to see OfCare working in the same way, with so many providers of services. The reality is that it just wouldn't work and would merely replicate some of the work currently performed by the Social Services Inspectorate and, latterly, by the Audit Commission. To some extent recent government initiatives have tried to address some of these variable policy and quality indicators with the launch of *Quality Protects*[9] and the work on key indicators that play an increasing role in SSI inspections.

Anyone who has had experience of local government in the last ten years would be loath to suggest that the future lies in another major re-organisation. One of the fundamental problems in childcare has been the constant changes which have affected social services departments . However, one of the central tenets of this piece is that, to a large extent, childcare is moving towards a new structure by default—through the contraction of local authorities, new lottery funding and the inexorable growth of the voluntary and private sector. To offset this it is necessary, at the very least, to present proposals which will counterbalance what is likely to happen if no constructive action takes place.

Three basic principles need to guide what is proposed: first, the necessity for a co-ordinated approach between central and local government, in the way services are planned and delivered; second, the desirability of some local autonomy which permits both involvement and variation in the way services are delivered; and, third, most importantly, a pooling of all of the resources of those agencies which serve children and their families.

If we are serious about creating a civil society, services need to be both flexible enough to accommodate local differences and yet have, at their heart, values and core services which could be expected throughout the whole of the UK.

The starting point must be the creation of a minister for children and family services within the Department of Health. Such an idea is not new and has been explored in a Gulbenkian-funded study *Effective Government Structures for Children*.[10] It is absolutely essential, if co-ordination is to take place at a local level, that it should be mirrored by similar co-ordination at central government level. The function of such a ministry is four-fold. First, to establish guidelines and minimum standards and to set budgets for child and family care services across the UK. Secondly, it would also organise the work of a National Childcare Inspection Unit (NCCI) which would be given powers to investigate all aspects of childcare, including health and education, where they impinge on social services, and recreation. The NCCI needs to have access to the Minister for Children and Family Services and to advise on the delivery of public childcare services both at local and regional level. Thirdly, a new National Childcare Research Unit (NCCR) should be allied to the NCCI. The NCCR would inform debate and policy by the publication of research data, statistical information and the establishment of those minimum standards which would be enforced across the UK. The NCCR should be given a powerful voice, with an obligation to report annually to parliament, through the designated minister. Lastly, the new ministry would liase with the next tier of community childcare services (CCCS), where service delivery would take place. What is aimed at is a national service which is both locally administered and able to deliver local priorities.

One cornerstone of the Children Act, 1989, which is frequently ignored, is its far-sighted recognition that public childcare is a responsibility not just of social services departments, but of the whole city, district or county-wide local authority. In practice this rarely happens. What is proposed is the establishment of CCCSs, coterminous with local authority and health boundaries, which would not only bring together all local authority departments concerned with children and their families, but also involve other services with responsibility for children.

Each CCCS would be headed by an elected chairman or woman, whose appointment would be ratified by the minister for children and family services. S/he would be charged with ensuring that the joint planning and providing roles of the CCCS were met and that local services achieved both the fulfilment of minimum standards and the acknowledgement of local conditions.

Representation on the CCCS would include all areas of local authority responsibility concerned with children, i.e. social services, housing (as it impacts on children and family services), recreation and education, health, the local magistracy, the voluntary and private sector and lay representation. It is essential that the lay representation should consist of local people who have some expertise or involvement in childcare issues, and that CCCSs should comprise both elected and co-opted members.

At an operational level, and responsible to the CCCS, would be a director who might come from various childcare backgrounds, such as education, social work or health. S/he would have statutory powers and responsibilities to submit returns, provide core services, chair the Area Child Protection Committee (ACPC) and take overall day-to-day management responsibilities for the delivery of childcare services at a local level. S/he would also be required to establish a local quality control and inspection unit to monitor services. Furthermore, s/he would direct the work of Community Childcare Teams (CCCTs). Each team would consist of representatives from social care or social work, special education, psychology, health and leisure. They would function like community mental health teams, in an integrated and multi-disciplinary way. Under this new model, the proposals for bringing together health and social services, in particular, might accord with the House of Commons Health Select Committee's declared wish to abolish the 'Berlin Wall' between the two services.

The significance of this proposed structure is two-fold. Firstly it involves all agencies concerned with children working together and, secondly, it embraces all aspects of children's care. For example, adoption services might be provided by the local authority or a voluntary agency and some services might appropriately be provided by the private sector. The aim would be the creation of mixed childcare teams (CCCTs) which would meet the needs of a particular locality. Its starting point is an holistic view of children which acknowledges that they need good health care, education, access to leisure and sport, reasonable housing and support for their families. Most local authorities, for example, run sports and leisure facilities that are well-used by children and their families, but such facilities are rarely seen alongside the public childcare system and consequently are not part of the equation of good childcare. However, their involvement in this process is essential if we are to build a structure which is not just for dysfunctional children. Quite often social services departments are involved in devising alternatives to custody schemes, or what used to be called intermediate treatment, which means the building of new recreational facilities, rather than the utilisation of existing resources. For the first time, it is proposed that all aspects of good care should be brought under the aegis of new local services. They could also be responsible for under-eight provision. At a local level they would provide the playgroups and nurseries that are part of the new government's initiative to extend comprehensive pre-school provision. Also part of the remit for any CCCS would be the provision of family housing, special services for children with disabilities and residential care for those children and young people deemed to require it. Equally important would be the need to make provision for special education, juvenile justice services, a range of community-based care such as family centres and drop-in care, recreation and sports and the development of local preventive services. At the other end of the age spectrum, each CCCS would link up with work proposals, aimed at providing employment for young school leavers. Because local authority representation on the CCCS would include social services, housing, the environment and leisure it might—for the first time—be possible to consider children's needs in their entirety.

Each CCCS would be expected to work in two ways. First, there would be a range of core services which all would provide, for example, access to education provision, child protection services, services for disabled children, child and adolescent psychiatry and juvenile justice services to the courts. Over and above this, considerable autonomy would rest within individual CCCSs to develop services to meet local needs. This approach would seek to develop communitarianism and the concept of a civil society through shared involvement. Furthermore, each area would be obliged to devote a pre-determined percentage of its budget to preventive childcare services. This would fit in with the Department of Health's drive to shift the emphasis in child protection work from investigative to family support services. The percentage would be set centrally and annually and each area would be required to report on how the money had been allocated.

At the core of any success would be the ability of the CCCSs to control hard won budgets and resources. To some extent the minister for children and family services would play a central role here; top-slicing education, where it impinges on social need, health, social services, leisure, child psychiatry and some general medical services to ensure that resources were available for allocation by the CCCS. Without this, the system would fail, perpetuating the same 'robber baron' concept, which maintains individual budgets and autonomous services. It would also prevent, at a local level, the nonsense of resources being identified for children, while no single department is prepared to meet the costs.

Lastly, the new structure allows for the possibility of local variation and the provision of voluntary or private sector services, without this developing, nationally, in an *ad hoc* way. It would be up to CCCTs to negotiate with voluntary organisations as to which services need to be developed. The current statutory duty to produce annual childcare plans would be strengthened. Furthermore, with CCCSs able to obtain services which fit in with local needs from local authorities, voluntary or private organisations, there is some possibility—at last—for comprehensive local services. And, of course, the multi-disciplinary nature of the local teams themselves would permit the real possibility of shared working.

To some extent, such a set of proposals plays upon developments which local authorities have made. Increasingly they recruit a senior officer, at assistant director level, responsible for children's services, attempting to build a childcare division within the wider social services budget. In other places, experiments have taken place to encourage joint organisational development. But it is doubtful that, if left to evolve, this would lead to the kind of wholesale restructuring which increasingly seems like the only way forward for a comprehensive childcare system.

But what of the costs? To a large extent what is proposed is a re-organisation and redistribution of existing services, but this does not mean that there would not be start-up costs. It is proposed that a single, one-off injection of lottery funding, perhaps from the New Opportunities Fund, should be used, to establish a UK-wide network of CCCSs in order to get the scheme established.

Such a scheme could provide a model of integrated childcare for other parts of Europe. It would also need to address both the training issues and also the economic elements of childcare, which the Chancellor, Gordon Brown, saw as the first rung of a comprehensive childcare strategy. But it would face head-on many of the concerns of a system which is failing children, young people and their families. The evidence is all too obvious: local authority social services are demoralised and often reduced to crisis services. Health, education and leisure facilities develop local projects with little regard for co-ordination, and a burgeoning voluntary sector is unwittingly helping to dissipate services even further. If we truly believe that children are, as Liv Ullman described them, the point of all movement, then they deserve co-ordinated services that will treat their needs holistically. What is proposed is nothing less than a service that will run high quality, nationally monitored, fostering, adoption, child protection and juvenile justice services, linked to health education, leisure, voluntary and private services. What greater task does any government have than to make the next generation the centre of its social policies?

Adoption and the Intolerant Liberal

Karen Irving

I WONDER whether Patricia Morgan's book would have been differently received if it had been published under the auspices of an institute perceived as left- rather than right-wing. The criticism from some seems at times to have little to do with the content, and rather more to do with the political stance of the reviewer.

It is always interesting to observe people who would regard themselves as liberal, open-minded and tolerant, being anything but. When I read a review of a recently published biography of Isaiah Berlin, the reviewer said that Berlin settled in the end for the most English of moral positions, that mutual tolerance is the greater part of liberty—a fact worth remembering when reviewing books published by a body with whom you do not necessarily share the same philosophy.

Sadly, mutual tolerance is not always evident in the world of adoption. It is a field of endeavour which arouses strong emotions and gives rise to strongly held views which all too often brook no dissent.

Recent years have seen little room for reflection on many issues. Contact with the birth-family, for example, was seen as a good thing no matter what the circumstances of the child, the birth-family or the adopters. Trans-racial placement was a bad thing, no matter what the view of the child, the birth-family or the adopters. I recall saying to Professor Murray Ryburn that his blanket prescription of open adoption did not always apply to our cases at Parents for Children. His response was that Parents for Children dealt with extreme cases and that generalised policies might not apply. Quite. I do not believe that Parents for Children deals with cases any more extreme than those of several other adoption agencies, and yet we are being faced with injunctions to follow a trend in the absence of any real research evidence on the *impact* of contact for the individual adopted child and his or her family.

Similarly, I would argue that the information we have from research is that children placed trans-racially do as well as other adopted children on all the usual measures. And as we know, adoption is, overall, a successful and positive outcome for children who cannot, for whatever reason, live with their birth-parents.

As it happens, I do not agree with some of the broad recommendations made by Patricia Morgan, but I do think she deserves a hearing. Several of her critics condemn her for calling for urgent action to tackle the problem of children drifting around care. They seem to see Morgan's arguments as coercing poor families to relinquish their children, preferably as babies, to adoptive families. Interestingly, a few months after Morgan's book was published, British Agencies for Adoption & Fostering, one of her critics, published *its* key findings—a research study of adoption statistics, based on the Department of Health 'Children Looked After' database.[1] BAAF urged new legislation to ensure that children in care are placed with adoptive families as quickly as possible. The BAAF study found that, of children adopted from care, 52 per cent came into care at the age of one year and just over half of these were under one month old. And yet Patricia Morgan has been berated for arguing that young children and babies who come into care are entitled to have adoption considered as a possible plan. She argues that several studies seem to show that once a child has been in care for six months, the likelihood of drifting around care is very high. Her observation is not new. It simply echoes the findings of Jane Rowe and colleagues years earlier.[2]

Endemic Delays

Patricia Morgan has argued that delays in adoption could be caused by current legislation, under which courts require councils to make sustained attempts to reunite children with their birth-parents. The BAAF adoption statistics project came to pretty much the same conclusion. Again, from the BAAF report:

> ... an analysis of the available adoption statistics suggests only a tiny number of babies are adopted annually, indeed the message given to prospective adopters is that children now needing adoption are older and present considerable challenges. The fact that half the adopted children in this study started to be looked after under the age of one and yet took so long to reach their permanent new families raises a number of questions ... Some delays may be accounted for by delays in court proceedings, for others there may have been attempted rehabilitation or complex planning issues with specific placement difficulties ... nevertheless, these delays are extremely worrying. This is a shocking set of statistics and should indicate the need for an urgent examination of what has happened to delay adoption of these children ... These findings suggest that the difficulties that some adopted children experience once placed are likely to have been aggravated by the delays they have experienced in care with placement moves and broken attachments. It is of considerable concern that so many children have experienced multiple moves in care. The potential impact of delay and frequent moves on the stability of placement and the need for increased post-placement support will be very substantial. This is particularly sad when these children come into care as infants with the potential for making good and lasting attachments ... The numbers of children admitted to care post-infancy (over the age of two years) who were adopted is remarkably small and declines even more rapidly for children aged over four years ... with only 153 of the children studied, starting to be looked after aged five years and over. These children waited the longest before they were adopted, on average five years. Given the increasing risk of disruption for older children, this length of time is of serious concern.[3]

Again, to echo Patricia Morgan's findings, the BAAF study identified a wide variation in the use of adoption between local authorities. These variations are not explained either by demographic differences or by availability of resources. The length of time between placement and finalising adoption also varies greatly between authorities.

> This variation can only be assumed to be due to a major difference in the use of adoption, reflecting a varying commitment to the priority that is given to adoptions as a means of securing permanent placements of children who cannot live with their birth families.[4]

The Need For Consistent Standards

Patricia Morgan recommends that adoption be transferred lock, stock and barrel from local authorities to voluntary agencies. It is understandable that she should say this. After all, the Department of Health Inspectorate has consistently found that it is the voluntary organisations which do most, but not all, of the most effective, innovative and creative work in the field of adoption and fostering. It needs to be remembered, however, that, prior to the 1976 Adoption Act, there had been scrutiny which found enormous variation in quality and standard of work done by adoption agencies, the majority of which were voluntary organisations. The 1976 Adoption Act was an endeavour to secure good and consistent standards throughout the country and it was thought that this would be better achieved by each local authority having a responsibility for adoption services in its area.

In my view, a mixed economy is best, preserving the best of the local authorities and the voluntary agencies. What is important is that the knowledge and skills needed for very complex adoption work should be available to a greater number of social workers than is the case at present. Training in adoption and fostering forms only one per cent of the social work training curriculum. And yet it is the field social worker holding responsibility for the child under the auspices of the local authority who is the crucial decision maker. Our experience at Parents for Children has been that it is sometimes the field social worker, who has no experience of adoption, who holds the power to agree or not to the adoption plan. Better training in adoption and more funding for it is an urgent need.

Patricia Morgan's examination of adoption pays no real attention to what it costs to operate a good adoption service. We at Parents for Children, and no doubt other agencies, have found that the post-placement and post-adoption support costs of the very damaged and complex children we now work with are very high. Our disruption rate is below five per cent, but year by year we jeopardise the agency's financial future by placing older traumatised children and by investing in the support services needed to help the adoptive family care for the child. We cannot charge a fee sufficient to cover our long-term costs. We are already seen as too expensive for some local authorities to refer children to us. We have sometimes offered to work for no fee at all when we have realised that a child finally referred to us after six or more years waiting for a family is about to be withdrawn because of the latest round of budget cuts in the local authority. We do not blame the hard pressed local authority. We do continually lobby for proper research to be undertaken on the cost/benefit analysis of adoption for children in care.

Summary

Criticism of Patricia Morgan's book seems to be fuelled by it being a publication from the Institute of Economic Affairs. One reviewer said that '... much of the work issuing from the Institute of Economic Affairs is an uneasy and volatile mix of the scholarly and polemical'.[5]

I hinted at the beginning of this article that to obtain real value out of studies and research we must seek not to be influenced by the author or the publisher, but to reflect on the underlying messages that emerge.

Adoption and fostering must surely be child-centred. If those in the childcare field are to truly respond to the needs of the individual child, then adoption and fostering agencies must be flexible, of high quality and under constant scrutiny. To achieve this, agencies, however they are managed or governed, must be adequately resourced with funds and appropriately skilled personnel.

Wanted: A Watchdog with Teeth

Liv O'Hanlon

PATRICIA Morgan's book came as a bolt of lighting. And as with bolts of lightning, some saw its illumination and others its danger. This volume sent shivers of recognition and gratitude through many of those who had seen adoption from the inside, because here was a careful and reasoned book confirming so forensically many of our worst fears and experiences. Meanwhile, the apologists for the status quo read trembling with apprehension as the catalogue of errors unfolded.

What the book did most importantly, brilliantly, was pull together research dating back years and form a picture of devastating clarity: a picture that showed the almost wilful neglect of children in the care system and the rise of ideas that had—perhaps simply because they were new—gained currency without any proof of their worth.

Adoption is not simple. It is—to pinch words from the marriage ceremony—a solemn and binding institution, not to be entered into unadvisedly, lightly or wantonly. It is the transference of a child to another family, forever and always, under the law, and it cannot—unlike marriage—be undone. This is no casual act.

There are good reasons to be cautious of adoption. You only have to look at the culpable stupidity and rank cruelty of the past to see why adoption has gained a questionable, if not utterly bad, name in some circles. The removal of children in the 1960s and 1970s on the sole ground of illegitimacy; the policy which took Aboriginal and Native American children from their families in Australia and the United States for no other reason than to cut them off from, as the white authorities saw it, their troublesome heritage; the forced migration of thousands shipped out to the colonies from children's homes; the stories of modern-day child-trafficking from poor to rich nations. Add to that the long-held beliefs of hiding adoption from children, of trying to eliminate their history, their birth-families, their sorrow, and it is easy enough to see why credence has been given to the anti-adoption propagandists.

But where they fail, for me, is to absorb the lessons of the past and look carefully at the present. We have, we are told often, a 'child-centred' system, where 'the best interests of children' prevail. We have, according to the fond claims of government ministers and adoption authorities, the best system in the world. But sometimes, to those such as myself who watch from the sidelines, these claims seem ominously hollow and terrifyingly self-deluding.

A Scandalous Past

Over the past two decades, scandal after scandal pointing the finger firmly at local authorities has erupted through the media, among them Pindown, Orkney, Cleveland and most recently Clywd and Merseyside. The voluntary sector doesn't escape accusation either: many independent children's charities have been implicated in the widespread abuse of children within their care.

Take the terrible injustices of child migration, a kinder name than mass trafficking which it surely could be termed given the economic overtones: up to 10,000 inmates of post-war children's homes were sent to the 'colonies'. No doubt the authorities said it was in their best interest. The last batch were shipped off in 1967. So who was culpable and has anyone been taken to task? Like so many other scandals, little has happened, even though a lot of people, including a 1998 Parliamentary Standing Committee, were shocked when they heard accusations that it had all been kept purposefully secret by the agencies and government officials involved. Not until the doughty Margaret Humphreys started to investigate in 1986 and produced a book in 1994[1] did the public get to hear of it. This episode does nothing for public confidence, particularly when it follows on so many scandals where social workers, including directors of social services found blameworthy in public investigations, have simply moved to other and often similar jobs.

What these scandals have produced is a cataract of reports overwhelming the territory of childcare with paper from the courts, local authorities, the voluntary sector, the police, the Department of Health's Social Services Inspectorate. Some, like the reports from the extraordinarily long-running Clwyd investigation, have never been allowed into the public arena. The report of the trubinal of inquiry into children's homes in North Wales, set up in 1996 by the Secretary of State for Wales and concluded in May 1998, is promised for publication, but no date has yet been set. One of the earlier reports had been suppressed because the insurance company providing cover for the local authority raised objections to publication, alarmed at the prospect of a massive payout. You can see why they might be alarmed, with the breadth of abuse in Clwyd, the separate Merseyside investigation of a further 74 children's homes, the Cheshire action and others, all of which may amount to up to 20,000 victims of abuse while in the public care.

Children 'Looked After'

While you try to ease your way round this cesspit, think too of the individual scandals such as those children killed while in social services' orbit—all the way from Maria Colwell to Rikki Neave. It isn't a pretty picture. And remember too, the children whose fate Patricia Morgan tracks so well, just the 'ordinary' kids in the 'looked-after' system. (What used to be know as the 'care' system is now called being 'looked after': one sad official misnomer following on another.)

As she points out, the situation for these 'ordinary' children in care is truly scandalous: bumping around between fosterers, in and out of care, back and forth to sad and inadequate families, delays about decisions, changes of addresses and schools and friends and loved ones and all, unsurprisingly, bringing on low levels of educational achievement, high levels of depression, teenage drug and alcohol abuse, prostitution, homelessness and a propensity to crime, prison and suicide. The figure quoted for England alone in 1998 is that there are 53,300 children looked after by local authorities and thus living away from home, but the figure has risen by eight per cent since 1994,[2] with an increasing percentage of non-voluntary care orders—i.e. where the parents do not agree with the decision to put their child/children into care. Then there are 32,000 on the separate child protection register, many of whom are still living at home.

These are only indications of the levels of cruelty and neglect suffered by those children who come to the notice of social services and of child protection workers willing to act. It is very hard to persuade the courts to issue non-voluntary care orders; the reasons have to be extremely well-founded. And while around one-third of children coming into care arrive without parental consent, it follows that the other two-thirds, around 18,000, are put into care by their parents, usually single mothers. It is this sector that the anti-adoption brigade get particularly uppity about; these are children who should not be separated permanently by adoption, they say, from their birth-mothers who love them dearly really.

The figure of 53,000 in care is a snapshot taken on one day in the year. The number of children looked after in England *at any time* during 1997/8 is estimated at 87,500.[3] Add in the children who do not qualify for the at-risk register or care but are on social services case lists, and the children involved in outreach plans run by voluntary bodies and other schemes, and you start to wonder just how many children are known by social workers to be living in less than adequate families.

Over the years we have seen reports, books, action plans, guidelines, legislation, press conferences and symposia. But what has it all done for the children? It is very hard to see if their lives have been eased at all, and very easy to feel despondent. In my more depressed moments I wonder whether there is any safe childcare to be had at all, or any way of making public care better. And it surely beggars belief that we are still told that our institutions deserve our trust and that we have the best system in the world.

The Forces Against Adoption

One of the more obvious answers—to some of us at least—is adoption. For one thing it works; even under the most undesirable circumstances its success rate is astounding. Secondly, it removes children from the care system that so badly fails them. It is hard to believe that, even if more risks were taken in adoption, that it could, *en masse*, fail children to quite such a degree as public care.

The trouble is that the weapons amassed by the anti-adoption forces through the good offices of past lunatic schemes such as the Aborigine and Native American adoption experience, the fight against 1960s sexual freedom and the convenience of shipping out your 'problem' children, are strong indeed. And they last in the public imagination, too.

Patricia Morgan outlines the history of adoption and the notions that surround it; that while its been around since the dawn of time, its reputation altered with the ages. The Victorians regarded adopton as a 'let out' for the wicked mother who had been sexually careless or economically imprudent. And the children marked out by the 'stain of illegitimacy' would surely only reveal 'bad blood' when the chips were down and punish anyone kind enough to take them in. These sentiments are still in part with us.

Then, in the middle of this century, came Bowlby and his disciples who told us that separation of biological mother and child was the worst thing that could ever happen. A theory or two, a spoonful of emotion, and suddenly we are all led to believe that all mothers love the child they have produced and all adopters are selfish and desperate, content to snatch other people's babies to lighten the burden of their infertility. So now all the hurt and blame is because of the adopters and the anti-adoption lobby now adds the accusation in a neat twist that the abiding cause of low numbers of adoptions is that adopters are so lacking in requisite qualities. Not, you understand, that public care has made any mistakes.

There is, too, the Children Act, 1989, with its concept of partnership with parents, which put in place the idea of endless attempts at family preservation, rehabilitation and restoration of children to the family. Clearly this is all very laudable and not to be dismissed lightly, but it is difficult not to see this partnership as dangerously undermining the cornerstone concept of 'the best interest of the child'. How much better it would be to have a partnership with the children instead, listen to them, cope with them, succour them, and provide them, if the circumstances demand, with what they most need—a functioning family.

In truth, social workers are right when they say it behoves us all—social workers, children, relinquishing parents, adopters—to prepare ourselves and be careful about what we're doing. These are not easy decisions. But we mustn't, surely, be so fearful of something going wrong, some chink of possible reconciliation left unattended, that nothing is done and children are left to falter and fail. The question that must remain at the forefront is: what will happen/would have happened to this child otherwise?

Far too often, for far too long, we have been told about the problems of adoption: that it creates difficulties of identity, that there is always a mental scar, that the only people to bring up a child are those who created him/her. Well, look at the alternative. A life in the care of the state perhaps, with its gruesome results.

Or a life back with a dysfunctional family. It is not fashionable to be, in social work jargon, 'judgmental' about inadequate families, and perhaps that's just as well because there are good reasons for the hopelessness of such families, the most obvious being that they derive from generations who have lived in similar circumstances. But the point about such families is that they are unlikely to provide a place of safety, love and stability for the growing child and unlikely to be helped to change sufficiently to do so. I'm not suggesting that such families be simply dumped, with no effort to ease their pain and desperation, but it's hard to offer up, on that idealistic altar of possible change, the children who will be ruined in their turn, if efforts fail.

It is not adoption that is the problem, it is what happens before adoption. There is an awfulness that comes with being unwanted in the first place; of being unloved; to suffer the infliction of mental and emotional pain; the torments of physical and sexual abuse; the horror of constant rejection. The nasty, inconvenient fact is that, whether or not any of us likes it, not all parents do love or want their children. This is from a mother in one of Professor Barbara Tizard's illuminating studies: 'I didn't want him, I did not want the responsibility of him, I wanted him adopted... Often he irritates me just being in the room...'[4] and so on. This child, taken into care, was given back to that mother at four, still unwanted. What madness controlled that decision? There seems to me to be a basic reluctance to believe that some mothers sometimes simply do not love their children and do not want them. Of course there are, as can be easily shown, many mothers who love their children hugely and yet are not able to care for them through, for example, illness and lack of wider family support. There are mothers who give up their children because they feel that they are, at that particular stage in their lives, not able to offer the devotion necessary at the time (some subsequently famous mothers at that: government minister Clare Short, MP Ann Keen, actress Pauline Collins).

There are mothers, particularly that generation of women in the 1960s and 1970s, who feel they were 'forced' to give up their children through social pressure and the stigma of illegitimacy. It is the loud and clear voice of those women speaking up over the past decade that has had such a powerful effect on adoption policy today: they were not ready or willing to give up their children. They loved their babies and feel the pain of separation every day since the baby was taken from them. These days, those women would have kept their infants and made good homes for them.

The difficulty is that those women have hijacked the adoption argument and distorted it. Children adopted these days are, in large part, children with a background of horror. They have suffered. They have not been loved, at least not in any readily understood way. They have been mutilated emotionally and, sometimes, physically. They desperately deserve another chance and they aren't going to get it from state care.

Where Do We Go From Here?

So what is to be done? Patricia Morgan is utterly right in following Schorr, Rowe and Tizard in their condemnation of long-term official care as a substitute for adoption. It should be avoided, clearly. I can only applaud when she states that adoption should and must become one of the first options for children who cannot live with their birth-parents, rather than the last resort. According to widely acknowledged research, a child who spends six weeks in continuous care is likely to stay long-term, so it would seem sensible at least to start thinking about adoption prospects at this stage. There are 37,800 children who have been 'looked after' officially for more than a year. Children linger on average for three years, eight months before adoption.[5] The system is managing only about 2,000 adoptions from care each year, and the figure is falling (see Table 1, p. 2). The system cannot, under these circumstances, be doing other than failing the children.

Patricia Morgan suggests a raft of reforms to tackle the problems of the system—delay and indecision in social services, the courts and the law. She firmly suggests removing local authorities from the adoption picture. She points out that child protection and adoption should be separate services; that it is difficult for local authorities to provide the specialist adoption service necessary; and that voluntary agencies would be better equipped to do the job. It is hard to take her to task on any of her suggestions.

But there's quite a bit else the system needs. If adoption went to the voluntaries, the voluntaries would have to expand, and who would they employ? People made redundant from local authorities, with all that implies. Certainly better management would help, and better supervision, but I have little real faith that the voluntaries would be able to offer a sufficiently changed system.

Social workers do not get a good deal: poor training, poor management often, and poor pay. They could do with a proper professional council with which they would be registered, as are doctors and nurses. There is no doubt that a great number of social workers do their damnedest to operate fairly and effectively, and do excellent work. Really. Those are the people who need the public's support; their status would be raised by such a council and the public's faith might be at least partially restored. And when things go wrong, social workers could be struck off and justice would seem to be done.

But there remain those unabashed by the present situation, both in local authorities and the voluntary sector, and their masters at the Department of Health. A small but significant indication of that lack of will to change radically can be seen in inter-country adoption (ICA). Mostly, local authorities ask voluntary agencies to assess couples for overseas adoptions, and the same problems prevail: too much bureaucracy, too much suspicion of adopters, and hugely negative attitudes to trans-racial and trans-cultural adoption. There is plenty of evidence showing that inter-country adoption works and that for children with few other options it can be a splendid solution. And to cap it all, there are international agreements that uphold the desirability of ICA within the protection of the law, common sense and humanity, agreements to which Britain is a signatory.

The new law on inter-country adoption, enacted this summer, revealed a lack of will within the Department of Health to change, whatever government may say openly and publicly. The DoH stated clearly that there was no intention to make overseas adoption easier and that it would enforce the retention of ICA by local authorities.

It seems to have passed the DoH by that most authorities want little to do with inter-country adoption. It is outside their expertise and outside what they understandably see as their responsibility. If ever there were a case for voluntary agencies, it would be in ICA. But the Department of Health has declared in the Act that, no, adoption is rooted in local authorities and that's where it stays. So, no real zeal for reform.

All of which is depressing and all of which points, for me, to one thing: a watchdog. Other countries have ombudsmen. It is not an original or untested idea; Norway has had one for 18 years. We need—desperately—a watchdog with teeth. Without it the *status quo* will remain the *status quo ante*. Nothing will shift. No amount of guidelines or rules will make an iota of difference without enforcement.

At present the system is to a great extent self-governing, but self-governing systems serve the governors, not the governed. Great bureaucracies need outside reviewers. Look again at ICA. The new law ratifies the Hague convention and thereby an office, known as the central authority (one each for England, Scotland, Wales and Northern Ireland) will act as the go-between among 'sending' and 'receiving' countries; it will govern the regulation and the day-to-day administration of international adoption. It could be a facilitator of good and swift practice, if it were properly defined, properly funded and extended to cover domestic adoption. But no extra money, facilities or ideas have been put in place. And yet here could be the nucleus of a wider office, a real central authority, a watchdog with teeth. An opportunity is being missed and, as a result, inter-country adoption, like domestic adoption, will continue to flounder in the prevailing anti-adoption culture.

We at the Adoption Forum do not believe that the sorely-needed change in attitude can or will come about without a sizeable change in administration. We want to see an independent authority, accountable to the public, covering both inter-country adoption and adoption within the UK. It could act, in fact, as the watchdog.[6] Without that watchdog, without those teeth, there is no one who will embarrass the authorities into action, listen to individual cases and change their course if necessary; who would count up the numbers of children in care and the numbers of adoptions from care, set league tables, rules, regulations and generally harass the system into working. Gas and electricity have their regulatory bodies. Surely children—our nation's future—deserve as much?

Secure Tender Loving Care As Soon As Possible, Please

Richard Whitfield

Our Child-Careless Society

MANY of those with long experience of working professionally with children and young people are deeply concerned about their contemporary emotional well-being and security. There are numerous anecdotes, and much scattered research which illuminate this. Here is a recent reflection of an experienced primary/middle school head-teacher, selected because it hints at the emotional heart of child welfare:

> It was a goal-setting period for year 8 children (aged 12+). The task was simple enough: 'Lie back, shut your eyes and imagine your future; then focus specifically on where will you be in five years time towards the end of your secondary schooling'.
>
> The answers saddened but did not surprise me. Many of the group were already predicting failure. One girl's fantasy imagination had her already dropped out of school but with a job as a hairdresser that she longed for. Hardly negative you might say, but it was only the start. The next fantasy picture covered up to age 21, the one after that to age 25. The girl lost her job, had a baby, and lost her boyfriend. It was all downhill. Despite the fact that she had got a job, she saw herself as a failure, relationally not even able to keep what she cherished.
>
> *More and more we have students without hope*. Teachers cannot take much of the blame for this. The powers that be seem unable to realise that there is a problem here that is deep-seated and emotional. It is an area that needs special training and skills. It is also an area that needs attention because, if the emotional climate is not right, then learning is blocked.

Few of this head-teacher's pupils have statemented 'special needs'. The school is in a typically middle-class neighbourhood, but the parenting of its children is, as elsewhere, often insecure and hard-pressed for sufficient attentive time, a phenomenon sometimes referred to as 'affluent neglect'.

The Home Secretary, Jack Straw, refreshingly tells us that parenting is the foundation of a stable society; sadly, few are yet serious about the political consequences of that sentiment. We have in fact become a child-careless society. We are ignoring much of the weight of evidence about child development in favour of adults' ideologies and practices which fail to respect children's needs for both the perception and experience of reliable love. Emotional security is the breeding ground for inner hope and self-esteem; without it, youngsters' brain development, identity, learning, reciprocity in relationships, mental health and much else within the potentials of genetic endowments are at risk, with often lifelong consequences. Official attitudes towards adoption are amongst the most serious aspects of the general malaise in polices affecting children and parents in the light of the many contemporary pressures militating against stability in family life.

The House of Commons Health Select Committee recently reported[1] on a lengthy and careful inquiry concerning the 51,000 children 'looked after' by local authorities. That is yet another depressing document concerning the appalling neglect and deprivation which these children suffer, both prior to and during their time within the care system, and of the huge risks to their emergence as adequate citizens. The enhancement of the now hugely diminished adoption option forms no part of the report's many costly recommendations for change.

The Audit Commission has drawn critical attention to the patchy performance of local authorities in services for people with special needs.[2] It was noted that there was a six-fold variation in the chance of 'looked-after' children having their homes moved three or more times per year, but again no mention of adoption as part of a cost-effective preventative strategy.

The Select Committee report referred to is being translated into targets and outcome indicators reflected in the Health Department document *Quality Protects*.[3] Again, there is no focus on adoption, but the concept of 'corporate parents' is introduced so as to encourage local authorities to 'act as any well-meaning natural parent would do towards their own child'. Here, as in the so-called 'childcare strategy' for employed parents, there is a failure to appreciate that children's core relational needs are mostly very particular. Reliable love for children can only be delivered by particular people who are fully, even irrationally committed to them in the long term. What, one might wonder, does the hug of a 'corporate parent' feel like to a distressed or tired child at bedtime?

No corporate state can deliver love directly to its children, but in executing its undeniable duty as a guardian it is charged with creating conditions through which particular others can so do. The corporate parent of all political and professional hues has been failing for some time. At best that 'parent' can only be an efficient facilitator and crisis intermediary. So we need now to be serious about the cultural encouragements and interventions which will transform 'looked-after' children into securely loved children.

A System In Need Of Legislative Revision

Adoption too often receives a bad press, as stories of poor social work practice, breakdown and unresolved birth-mother grief are deemed more newsworthy than success. Yet adoption is arguably the touchstone for a nation's real concern for its children. Patricia Morgan's book[4] was a timely and welcome contribution to the very necessary debate to review and markedly upgrade the status of adoption in Britain. In extending the widespread concern of many, the book has gathered much of the relevant detail. Nobody in public office concerned with child welfare should now be complacent about the current situation, and adoption must re-emerge as a serious option.

The present system is essentially one of an unreformed monopoly. In far too many cases, the state has proved to be an unreliable, neglectful and often wasteful parent. Yet, in a decent democracy, conscious of the rights and needs of the most vulnerable, some real guardianship beyond the immediate family system has to be exercised. In the hands of local authorities and their often hard-pressed and inadequately trained social workers, that guardianship has proved to be grossly ineffective as far as many children are concerned. Insiders know that some local authorities lose track of some children on their care books. One paediatric consultant from Cheshire despairingly noted in a press letter in 1997:

> I meet children of ten years old who have had ten foster homes since they were aged five. My record is a 14 year-old with 20 moves. Many such children can attach to no-one. They run off and get lost.

I recently heard of a four-year-old white boy without physical handicap who was handed by his last local authority to a national voluntary agency after 12 moves. Unsurprisingly, by this time he had a range of behavioural difficulties. Such examples hardly do credit to the Children Act, 1989, which is deficient with respect to the need for early secure arrangements for all children. Legislative change has therefore become imperative.

Given the wealth of evidence which shows the generally very successful outcomes of adoption, along with the newer findings of developmental brain research and of studies of human attachment, the obstructiveness, rigidity, and above all tardiness of our adoption system has become an increasing scandal. For example, a mere ten per cent of children under 16 in local authority care presently 'become available' for adoption. As one 14-year-old once asked me: 'Why is it that everywhere I go government pays money, and someone gets money to stop me having a real Mum and Dad?'

The core headings for the answer to that pointed question are:

- The anti-adoption bias in pregnancy counselling
- The misuse of the foster-care system
- Overload and confusion of social services roles
- Uninvolved natural fathers
- Misapplication of the ethnicity and other 'matching' variables
- Ineffective data bases for facilitating placements
- A cultural underestimating of the resources, resilience and skills required for both past and contemporary lone parenting[5]

Draft legislation to update adoption law has now been in the wings since 1996, delayed due to cross-party political timidity. Given the inadequate local authority response to central social work 'guidance', something much more radical is now necessary. This chapter is a contribution to that end. It dwells on some key first principles about taking all our children seriously, notes three recent studies of adoption outcomes, and gives an outline of the remit for a proposed new independent adoption authority through whose work we might expect a significant reduction in high-cost residential and foster care in favour of generally much earlier adoption. My proposals also give a more central role to health personnel, and especially health visitors, with a reduction of the overall influence of social workers.

Political Will

Partly through fear of controversy about the desirability of gay and lesbian adoptions, a marginal yet normative issue, the political will to introduce new legislation has been lacking. Furthermore, media interest in the unresolved grief of a handful of birth-mothers has detracted from the extensive good news which remains appropriately and unobtrusively embedded in the reality of many tens of thousands of adoptees' lives. Two recent ministers of state in different administrations, John Bowis and Paul Boateng, have tried to secure relevant professional change through sharper administrative guidance from the central Social Services Inspectorate to local authority social services departments. Such manifestly sensible guidance is often not followed, and in practice is unenforceable.

In addition to the longstanding location of a small adoption office within the Department of Health, government now has a cross-departmental Social Exclusion Unit. The enhancement of adoption as a respected childcare option should be a proper part of its agenda in building up contemporary political momentum within 'joined-up government'. Social exclusion, a basket term covering behavioural features which demonstrate as early as the primary school years little allegiance to social membership and responsibility, generally has its origins in early childhood insecurity and stressed, inattentive or abusive parenting. Such features are both expensive and difficult to reverse.

As I was writing the draft of this chapter there were yet again problem cases in the headlines. An apparently loving foster-parent couple (the Bramleys) were driven to the desperation of eloping to Ireland for four months with two three- and five-year-old children in their care. Their local authority social services department (one with a markedly tarnished professional record) intended to remove the children from the couple's home, and reverse its original intention to support the couple's application for adoption, despite the birth-mother's support for that course of action. A *Times* leader noted:

> The unpredictable prejudices, petty political correctness and dithering which commonly pervade childcare legislation and practice have contributed to a sharp decline in the number of adoptions... If the high profile Bramley case is not resolved quickly, decisively and transparently, yet more prospective parents may decide that it is more trouble than it's worth to foster or adopt.[6]

The Bramleys' action gained huge public sympathy. The family went through some unique intervening experience during which they are likely to have bonded strongly in the face of a perceived aggressor. Fortunately, on 23 June 1999, the High Court determined that the two children should stay with the Bramleys until the spring of 2001, sharing legal parental responsibility with Cambridgeshire County Council. At that point an adoption application by the couple will be considered, making the case a protracted one, possibly in order to discourage others who might contemplate such extreme action in order to assert the child's early right to security. Whatever the final outcome, this case suggests that the present rule book on adoption law, such as it is, needs to be rewritten.

Reliable Love Brings Early Nurture, And More, And For All

None of us ask to be born, and none of us choose our birth-parents. Likewise, children are not essentially a consumer choice; they become first the responsibility rather than the 'property' of their parents. Through whatever circumstances children arrive in a household, they are precious gifts. A caring society must, however, take all its 'seed-corn' children seriously regardless of the parental lottery, and that is a matter of evidence-informed values,[7] and reliable public guardianship.

I have fairly recently asked varied groups of teenagers to use their retrospective imaginations to find a few words for what they would have liked to say to the world immediately after being born. Their responses (following) are very telling. (Readers might pause here also to try the exercise.)

Youngsters' responses in face-to-face discussion essentially fall into two categories: orders or requests, and questions, with significantly more of the former:

Orders/Requests		**Questions**
Cuddle me	Comfort me	Who are you?
Keep me warm	Just accept me	Who is my Dad?
Look at me	Play with me	Where am I?
Give me fresh air	Listen to me	Who do I belong to?
Feed me	Protect me	Why am I here?
Clean me up	Love me	What's going on?

Sometimes youngsters have simply offered a greeting such as: 'Hi! I'm here', or 'Hello Mum', while occasionally there is the plea: 'Hope you approve'.

Such responses reflect our timeless intuitions of deep need, and require widespread expression in our rituals, priorities and practices of child nurture. To one reflective 14-year-old boy 'Love me' meant 'All those other things which my mates have suggested about what baby wants, given automatically and without my asking'. It would be hard to find a better definition of 'unconditional love'.

Too often we fail to act upon the firm knowledge that infants need to experience unconditional love which grows from consistently sympathetic attention. If we are not so treated, and persuaded of our wonderfulness when we are small, later on it will be much harder for anyone to persuade us that we are valuable, and that life in society is and can be generally satisfactory. In such circumstances we will soon be awkward, angry, uncooperative, sad and depressed, then perhaps violent. Within a woundedness of spirit we become unattractive to the world, which then tends to become even less responsive to our needs. We become, at worst, severely distrusting, defiantly detached, unfeeling, rootless, lost, unlovely and unlovable. These are in many ways *rational* responses to our experienced emotional neglect in which our faint infantile hopes of a good-enough feel for life have been dashed.

The emerging empirical findings prompted by attachment theory are important for human welfare as a whole. From the point at which the fertilised ovum becomes attached to the uterine wall, human life begins. Overlaid upon genetic endowments, attachments and separations shape identity thereafter. Secure attachment patterns in infancy to psychologically available and committed parents, or parent-substitutes, seem the strongest single environmental predictor of future human wellness and capability assessed by the variety of forms of 'intelligence',[8] including IQ,[9] which are relevant to creating reciprocal social life.

Secure infant/parent attachments build up the infants' trust in the world, bestow an early sense of self-worth, create the confidence for safe exploration, and endow skills of appropriate response within other later relationships. Both secure and insecure attachments in the early stages of life, which are affected greatly by parental behaviours and circumstances, have a high (80 per cent) probability of transmission between generations. So, as we all intuitively know, drifting or harsh circumstances in children's early lives have long-term consequences.

In non-clinical (i.e. 'ordinary' population) samples of 'westernised' infants, no more than about 60 per cent appear to become securely attached to a parent figure by the age of three years. Insecure attachments (sub-classified by researchers in carefully planned observation studies as 'avoidant', 'resistant/ambivalent', and 'disorganised'), appear in 90 per cent of cases in samples of clinically referred young patients, there being highly significant associations with measures of anti-social behaviour, including criminality.[10]

Sound attachment-promoting behaviour by parents demonstrates what I have earlier termed 'reliable love'. This has essentially a 'covenant' nature. It combines practical commitment, psychological resources and an ability of the loving carer to 'get into youngsters' shoes'. The value of this external commitment, perceived by the child in the everyday, becomes a deeply embedded sense for the child concerning the intrinsic worth of its own separate self. The child being lavished with care, and in general responding appreciatively to it, begins to sense its own value, and that is the very basis of social trust.

Ensuring that baby, infant, child, adolescent is in general treated with sensitive consideration ensures that he or she becomes 'authored'. In so many ways we are all nobodies, and cannot become reasonably adjusted people without at least one committed somebody. Persons are not 'islands', but social, relational, and interdependent. Infants' sense of hope is mirrored from birth in the reflective countenance and nurture of others, particularly mothers in the first 18 months to two years of life, who are regularly and reliably close by. Babies do not know that they have faces until they 'find' another interested and warm one to respond to, so as to start the long journey towards having an identity. (Hence it is preferable if the early faces which they see are neither stressed nor depressed.)

Recent brain research[11] is demonstrating that tender loving care early in the life course affects the complex neural wiring of the developing infant brain, which increases its weight about four-fold during the first year of life. The brain's intellectual and social capacities are in important ways driven by an emotional centre, the 'amygdala'. If potential neural circuits permitting considerate responses from the child are not formed and used by the age of eight to ten years, then the individual is likely to be permanently impaired in terms of both compassionate and ethical behaviour.

Thus the emerging data from attachment and neurological studies is giving the very clear signal that early life, with its significant vulnerabilities and fluidity of the emotional mind, is a uniquely precious window of opportunity. The implications of this go far beyond adoption, and need to sensitise our priorities concerning parental availability and caring skills more widely.

An Update Concerning Adoption's Positive Outcomes

Patricia Morgan's book[12] gives insights into some of the evidence concerning adoption's outcomes from the children's point of view. Compared with likely alternative family structures, the trends are both generally consistent and impressive. Very recent papers have added further weight.

Data from the National Child Development Study (which takes as its base a cohort of over 17,000 children born in one week during March 1958) has been used[13] to examine variables in school achievement and adult qualifications amongst adoptees, non-adopted children from similar birth circumstances, and other members of the cohort. The adoptees (75 per cent of whom were in 1958 placed in the first three months of life, in contrast to the mean age of about eight years in the trickle of current adoptions) performed significantly better than ex-nuptial children who had remained with their birth-mothers on tests for reading and mathematics at age seven, and of general ability at age 11. Furthermore they retained this advantage in both school-leaving and adult qualifications recorded by age 33. Measures of the educational environment of the home, and of parental interest in education, emerged more strongly than socio-economic circumstances as central predictors of these variations, suggesting that a climate of encouragement and support is more important than affluence. The ex-nuptial children of this study who remained with their natural mothers had 'a cumulative disadvantage across childhood', with relatively high rates of emotional and behavioural problems.

The first phase of a study[14] of developmental catch-up and deficit following the adoption within the UK of nutritionally and socially early-deprived children from Romanian orphanages has shown a spectacular degree of intellectual progress by the age of four, with the age of orphans' entry to the UK being the most decisive factor in the level of improvement. The duration of privation in Romania during the first two years of life was found to be a more important predictor of cognitive outcome than levels of privation assessed by and associated with malnutrition. This suggests that psychological privation (from, for example, lack of play and communicative experiences) which is early addressed by the onset of reliable love and care can be markedly corrected. By age four no measurable deficits in relation to normal populations were discernible amongst the children who came to the UK before the age of six months. However, the researchers suggest that it now seems likely that some persisting deficits will remain for those children who came to the UK after their first birthday. In short, the prescription, yet again, seems to be *'tender loving care as soon as possible please'*.

If we look for useful comparable data from overseas, a carefully executed longitudinal study[15] of a cohort of 1,265 children born in New Zealand in 1977 has reported on a wide range of outcome measures, confirming that adoption confers a degree of childhood advantage. On eight outcomes covering the early childhood phase to age five, and six beyond that to age 15, children in adoptive families fared marginally better than natural children in two-parent family settings. Those reared in lone-parent families had in general fared much less well than those in the two other 'intact' family types, with the significant statistical differences being impressively or, rather, depressingly constant over all 14 outcomes. This finding simply confirms the wealth of survey data (which cannot be applied directly to individual cases) demonstrating, in the words of a recent authoritative review, that:

> The family environment with the fewest risks for unsuccessful child socialisation is an harmonious, intact two-parent family. Children are at risk for developing problems in adjustment when they grow up in either a (regularly) conflicted two-parent or a single-parent home.[16]

The New Zealand study sensibly concludes that:

> while it would be unwise to return to a situation in which all single mother's are advised that it would be in their child's best interests if the child was placed for adoption, there is still a place for adoption as a child welfare provision which protects the interests of children. In particular, the present results suggest that in situations in which there are identifiable and serious concerns about the ability of biological parents to provide adequate care for their children, adoption is likely to be in the child's best interests.[17]

Aside from adoption's positive impacts upon children, *birth-mothers* who have had their offspring adopted later demonstrate several significant life advantages.[18]

Amongst these are:

- Higher educational aspirations and achievements into adulthood.
- Lower rates of depression than among lone mothers.
- Greater employment participation and less dependency one year beyond childbirth compared with lone mothers.

- Less likelihood of repeating ex-nuptial pregnancy.

So there is evidence to support the hope that adoption tends to enable single birth-mothers having unsought pregnancies to 'make a new start'.

Advice Upon Pregnancy

Superficial moral and practical judgements about family types are generally unhelpful to the public debate concerning children. However, the present cultural situation, in which planned lone parenthood is not discouraged, abortion is freely available and adoption considered, if at all, as the last resort for children, is unsatisfactory. For birth-mothers without reliable cohabiting partners the social stigma (in all cases unhelpful to the child) has sadly shifted onto those who might consider having their children adopted early in life. Adoption clearly exposes a range of ambivalences which our society demonstrates towards pre-term life, children, parents and partnering.

There is no legal obligation on medical advisers, the most influential front-line group, nor on social workers, to offer and explain the adoption option to biological parents who cannot, seem unlikely to, or do not wish to, cope with the long-term practical consequences of their pregnancy. This is a major weakness in abortion-related advice, and the 'quick fix' abortion is beguiling in its apparent simplicity.

Due to the marked fall in adoption's prevalence there is now widespread ignorance about the option. It has therefore become necessary to ensure that, in the processes of pre (and post)-natal work, the possibility of adoption is explained to all pregnant women who have unsought or 'inconvenient' pregnancies. This would not be to bring undue and improper pressure upon pregnant women, but would merely ensure that they are sensitively informed about all options and their possible or likely consequences.

Here is not the place to discuss abortion and its psychological and general health costs, but there is little doubt that some women would choose adoption rather than abortion if it were sympathetically explained to them. Arguably, medical and paramedical staff have that moral obligation, which includes discussing the phenomenon of long-term abortion bereavement, if women's considered choices are to be fully honoured. The process being advocated is consistent with a long-term preventative health strategy.

Some Proposals Involving Health Visitors And A New 'Adoption Authority'

The need for new practical initiatives on the legislative front and beyond which do more than update and tinker with the present system is now clear. This has been implicitly recognised by Jack Straw as Home Secretary and Chairman of the Ministerial Group on the Family in a speech to the Family Policy Studies Centre on 25 January 1999. Aspects of the Children Act, 1989 will also need to be amended so that the impression of adoption as a procedure of last resort is clearly corrected.

In its welcome first paper on family policies,[19] which deferred discussion of adoption for 'separate' treatment, the present government has emphasised its desire to enhance the role, status, and therefore presumably training, of health visitors in family and parenting matters. Given the longstanding and widespread public confidence in the practice of most health visitors, there is clearly much that is good in their professional traditions to build upon. Crucially, health visitors, unlike social workers, see a representative cross-section of early parenting.

In the five following proposals, well-trained health visitors, seen as increasingly expert in the norms of early child development, are given a major statutory role in being the independent guardians of infants' interests, with an obligation both to suggest and to recommend adoptions, making, as soon as practicable, appropriate referrals to specially approved regional adoption agencies. Most such referrals, including a medical commendation, would, of course, be with parental consent. This should reduce substantially the risk of non-specialist social work vacillation and unhelpful local authority ideologies. Nonetheless, measurably inadequate or uncommitted parents should be given strict time limits to amend their ways so as to minimise the likely damage to the child in what is, in reality, a psychological emergency.

I have considerable sympathy with Patricia Morgan's call[20] for adoptions to be arranged only via specialist voluntary sector bodies, even though at least a few local authorities have shown both a commitment towards and expertise in adoption. Whatever the future administrative mechanisms, medical and placement agency staffs' training, values, research-informed beliefs, expertise and experience will be key factors in facilitating placements.

An open tendering mode for adoption service contracts, emphasizing collaborative inter-agency practices and specialist expertise in adoption work, needs to be instituted. This should be on a regional basis under the aegis of a new independent adoption authority whose core funding should be met by central government. The council of that body should be non-party political, widely representative, including appropriate lay appointees, but should exclude those for whom adoption is ideologically problematic.[21]

The new adoption authority would operate in a changed legal context for all new-borns. It should include:

1. Obligatory links initiated by all birth-parents of new-borns, or others acting on their behalf, to the services of a registered health visitor. This could be an additional aspect of the present procedure for registration of the birth. Health visitors, working as appropriate in liaison with GPs, paediatricians, and child psychologists attached to health teams, would have a duty to monitor all infant welfare both pre-term and over the first year of life. In cases of doubtful developmental thriving, confirmed by a GP or paediatrician, the health visitor support and surveillance would remain for at least a second year. In cases of unresolvable relationship tensions between parents and their designated health visitor, parents would have an option to change their health visitor once. If moving home to another district, parents of under-threes would have the duty to transfer to a parallel service. Proper collaboration with the child health services could, as in France, be a condition for receipt of social security payments, including child benefit. Good practice would ensure that carefully supervised health visitors would arrange to see the parent(s) pre-term, and then no less than once a month in the case of first-born children.

However, within a team framework, health visitors should be given wide discretion, thoroughly realistic case-loads and remuneration commensurate with their qualifications, responsibilities and experience as the first line of preventative defence of children's interests. The potential benefits for all children and their carers, and the long-term savings to taxpayers, would more than justify the necessary investment. Coherent investment in early child development makes good sense from every angle, and local health teams are central to that.

2. An expectation that contracted adoption agencies would become aware of likely adoption cases, through the health visitor-based referral system, before the end of the first year of life. These agencies would have an obligation to facilitate adoption orders in the courts as soon as possible, and only in exceptional cases after the child's second birthday. Agency contracts would be monitored for speed, sensitivity and thoroughness of service, and all would be required to offer, possibly through consortia arrangements, a post-adoption service for adoptees, their legal and birth-parents.

3. Those children who, for whatever reasons, become available for adoption later than the second year of life, with referrals as at present from a variety of sources, must have their cases resolved within 12 months of agency notification. This will demand an appropriate responsiveness from agencies and the court system, with judges specialising in children's work being able to censure those responsible for avoidable delay.

4. Agencies operating in the field of foster care would be required to justify to a child placement review panel, presided over by a judge, the cases of all children under the age of 16 who have been in foster care for more than one year, and to do so annually. Panels, which should include at least one lay member with experience of adoption as a parent or child, would have the right to commend and secure adoptions, taking into account all relevant factors of case history.

5. The adoption authority would manage a confidential national register of approved adopters, and, collaborating with government, would remove financial and other disincentives to local

authorities working openly with the voluntary sector. Local authorities would be required to remit classified statistics concerning all children under the age of 16 in need of permanent substitute care from their areas. This would enable the adoption authority to publish in the public interest a quarterly 'National Child Placement Statistical Bulletin'.

The intent of these proposals is to ensure that all children have viable, 'good enough' parents as soon as possible in their lives. Where new parents' skin colour, or other physical features, or other aspects of social and genetic background, do not match the birth variables, we should worry far less than much social work practice has presumed. At all times, case practice should presume the probability of a partly hidden 'psychological emergency' as far as the child is concerned.

Adoption Works

All children need to grow up in affectionate environments which are neither excessively unpredictable nor multiply stressed. Loving arms in childhood, most appropriately from two collaborating parents of differing genders, which mould around the child's specific developmental, temperamental and physical needs, are the best guarantee of human happiness, sound citizenship and much else. This has to become the much more explicit normative foundation for public policies for children. We have reaped too much sad and avoidable insecurity and social deviance from other emphases which still dominate a politically correct but wrong-headed agenda.

Adoption generally enhances the emotional, physical, and intellectual capacities of the children who are adopted. It is likely to improve the life chances of the biological mother. It saves vast amounts of money for the taxpayer in a range of spheres, and adds value to our national human resources. It also brings much happiness to adopting parents. As a serious option in child welfare it is good for society.

Reliable love, amid sufficient material support and educational encouragement, seem to be all that really matter in child development. It is now our moral duty to secure those provisions for all children, not only through reformed adoption policy and practice, but through far more pervasive family policies. While such policies require life-cycle sensitivity, the early years of life are, in the recent words of a senior consultant paediatrician:

> absolutely crucial to the development of children's bodies, minds and personalities. Deprivation in early life causes life-long damage, delinquency and despair.[22]

The collective guardianship duty now required to better safeguard all our children must find due expression in adoption policies. These must have a greater sense of urgency so as to impact many more children in need early in their lives, for early attachments have life-long consequences.[23]

Notes

Patricia Morgan

1 See, for example, Schorr, A., *Children and Decent People,* London: Allen and Unwin, 1975.

2 Benet, M.K., *The Character of Adoption,* London: Jonathan Cape, 1976, p. 20.

3 Shawyer, J., *Death by Adoption,* Auckland, NZ: Cicada Press, 1979.

4 Musick, J.S., Handlet, A. and Waddill, K.D., 'Teens and adoption: a pregnancy resolution alternative', *Children Today,* November/ December 1984, p. 26.

5 Howe, D., Sawbridge, P. and Hinings, D., *Half a Million Women,* Harmondsworth: Penguin, 1992, p. 154. p. 101.

6 Fratter, J. *et al.*, *Permanent Family Placement*, London: British Agencies for Adoption and Fostering, 1991, p. 10.

7 Department of Health, 'Adoption services in three London Local Authorities', *Adoption: In the Child's Best Interest*, London: HMSO, 1991, p. 14.

8 Dance, C., *Focus on Adoption: A Snapshot of Adoption Patterns in England-1995*, London: British Agencies for Adoption and Fostering, 1997. Estimates were based on a survey of 45 per cent of English local authorities.

9 *For Children's Sake: An SSI Inspection of Local Authority Adoption Services,* Social Services Inspectorate, Department of Health 1996.

10 Dance, *Focus on Adoption, op. cit.*, p. 12.

11 Benson, P.L., Sharma, A.R. and Roehlkepartain, E.C., *Growing Up Adopted*, Minneapolis: Search Institute, 1994, p. 78.

12 Fitzgerald, J., *Understanding Disruption*, London: British Agencies for Adoption and Fostering, 2nd edn., 1990.

13 Lambert, L. and Streather, J., *Children in Changing Families,* London: Macmillan, 1980. Ninety-three per cent of the children in the National Child Development Study who were adopted as babies were still with their adoptive families at 11.

14 Thoburn, J. and Rowe, J., 'A snapshot of permanent family placement for children', *Adoption and Fostering*, Vol. 12, No. 3, 1988; also Fratter, J., Rowe, J., Sapsford, D. and Thoburn, J., *Permanent Family Placement*, London: British Agencies for Adoption and Fostering, 1991.

15 The Essex Specialist Family Placement Service found that approximately one in five children had left placements two and a half years later. Wedge P., 'Family finding in Essex', in Wedge, P. and Thoburn, J. (eds.), *Finding Families for 'Hard-to-place' Children: Evidence from Research*, London: British Agencies for Adoption and Fostering, 1986. A lower disruption rate of 11.3 per cent for 335 'special-needs' children from care has been recorded for the Lothian home-finding teams (or 4.6 per cent for those aged under ten at placement, and 21.7 per cent for those ten or over). O'Hara, J. and Hoggan, P., 'Permanent substitute family care in Lothian: placement outcomes', *Adoption and Fostering*, Vol. 12, No. 3, 1988. However, a follow-up study on 194 of the children reported that 20.6 per cent had disrupted by five years. Borland, M., Triseliotis, J. and O'Hara, G., *Permanency Planning for Children in Lothian Region*, University of Edinburgh, 1990.

16 For example: Witmer, H.L., Herzog, E., Weinstein, E.A. and Sullivan, M.E., *Independent Adoptions: A Follow-up Study*, Beverley Hills: Russell Sage Foundation, 1963. This involved 484 children about nine years after placement, and data from the adoptive parents, teachers and psychological testers. This described the outcomes for two-thirds of the children as 'excellent to fair', and a quarter as 'definitely unsatisfactory'.

17 Crellin, E., Pringle M.K. and West, P., *Born Illegitimate: Social and Economic Implications*, Windsor, England: NFER, 1971; and Seglow, J., Pringle, M.K. and Wedge, P., *Growing Up Adopted*, Slough: National Foundation for Educational Research in England and Wales, 1972.

18 Lambert, L., and Streather, J., *Children in Changing Families*, London: Macmillan, 1980. The sample now included 294 children who had been born illegitimate and not adopted and 115 adopted children. A problem with longitudinal studies are the losses over time, due to death, emigration, refusals and inability to trace earlier respondents. While a third of the adopted children were lost to the Study, analysis showed that the results were unlikely to be biased through non-response.

19 *Ibid.*, p. 131.

20 St. Claire, L. and Osborn, A.F., 'The ability and behaviour of children who have been "in care" or separated from their parents', *Early Child Development and Care*, Vol. 28, No. 3, 1987.

21 Twelve per cent were highly attached to the father only; 18 per cent were highly attached to the mother only. On some measures, attachment rates were slightly lower than for non-adopted siblings, but nowhere did this exceed ten per cent lower, and there was no statistical significance.

22 Based on a national USA sample of 47,000 adolescents from the public school system, Benson, P., *The Troubled Journey: A Portrait of 6th-12th Grade Youth*, Minneapolis: Search Institute, 1993.

23 *Ibid.*, p. 60.

24 Maughan, B. and Pickles, A., 'Adopted and illegitimate children growing up', in Robins, L. and Rutter, M. (eds.), *Straight and Devious Pathways from Childhood to Adolescence*, Cambridge: Cambridge University Press, 1990, p. 41.

25 Raynor, L., *The Adopted Child Comes of Age*, London: Allen and Unwin, 1980.

26 They had fostered for the Thomas Coram Foundation, or adopted though the National Adoption Society. The original total of 288 families was reduced to 160 (56 per cent of the original sample) due to those who had died, emigrated, could not be found, or refused to take part. Background information suggested that those who were interviewed were much like the original overall group. Indeed, where one of a dyad refused, it seemed that is was the satisfied adopters, or adoptees from satisfied families, who were more likely not to want their children or themselves interviewed.

27 Maughan and Pickles, 'Adopted and illegitimate children growing up', *op. cit.*

28 Hodges, J, and Tizard, B., 'IQ and behavioural adjustment of ex-institutional adolescents', *Journal of Child Psychology and Psychiatry* Vol. 30, No 1, 1989, p. 54.

29 Kadushin, A., *Adopting Older Children*, New York: Columbia University Press, 1970. The 91 families involved accepted a total of 117 children for adoption. The agency concerned had placed 150 children in the first instance, but 12 placements failed, leaving 138 cases and 112 families. Of these 112 families, 17 could not be contacted and 4 refused—a low rate for adoption follow-up research of 4.2 per cent.

30 Groze, V., *Successful Adoptive Families: A Longitudinal Study of Special Needs Adoption*, Connecticut: Praeger Westport, 1996.

31 Berry, M. and Barth, R.P., 'Behaviour problems of children adopted when older', *Children and Youth Services Review*, Vol. 11, 1989, pp. 221-38. This study involved 900 cases of older-child, special-needs adoptions: 60 per cent had been physically abused, 80 per cent were neglected and 33 per cent sexually abused; also Reid, W.J., *et al.*, 'Adoptions of older insitution-alised youth', *Social Casework,* March 1987, pp. 140-49.

32 Irving, K., Director, *Parents for Children*, personal communication, July 1997.

33 Thoburn, J., *Success and Failure in Permanent Family Placement*, Aldershot: Avebury, 1990.

34 Triseliotis, J. and Russell, J., *Hard to Place: the Outcome of Adoption and Residential Care*, London: Heinemann Educational Books, 1984.

35 Just under a half of those identified were able to be traced and interviewed. Background comparisons by sex, socio-economic status, age at care, numbers of moves before placement, nature of original families, recorded problems etc., revealed no difference between those interviewed and those 'lost'. Those who did not want to take part may have done better, or worse, or the same as those interviewed. Obviously, those who underwent 'care' experiences may wish to put their unfortunate pasts behind them, or the inadequate may lead the kind of marginal existence which makes them impossible to track.

36 Triseliotis and Russell, *Hard to Place*, *op. cit.*, p. 90.

37 Wolkind, S.N. and Renton, G., 'Psychiatric disorders in children in long-term residential care: a follow-up study', *British Journal of Psychiatry,* Vol. 135, 1979, pp. 129-35. Also a survey of children from over 2,000 institutions in the USA,

ten years before, found that three-quarters were thought to be emotionally disturbed. [Peppenfort, D.M. and Kilpatrick, D.M., 'Child rearing institutions, 1966; selected findings from the first national survey of children's residential institutions', *Social Service Review* Vol. 43, No. 4, pp. 448-59.]

38 Triseliotis and Russell, *Hard to Place, op. cit*., p. 78.

39 Rutter, Quinton and Hill, 'Adult outcome of institution-reared children: males and females compared', in Robins and Rutter, *Straight and Devious Pathways from Childhood to Adolescence, op. cit.*

40 Benson, P.L., Sharma, A.R. and Roehlkepartain, E.C., *Growing Up Adopted*, Minneapolis: Search Institute, 1994, p. 43.

41 Thoburn, J., *Success and Failure in Permanent Family Placement*, Aldershot: Avebury, 1990, p. 18.

42 Barth, R. *et al*., 'Contributions to disruption and dissolution of older-child adoptions', *Child Welfare*, Vol. 65, 1986, pp. 359-71; and Festiger, T., *Necessary Risk: A Study of Adoption and Disrupted Adoption Placements*, New York; Child Welfare League of America, 1986.

43 Cohen, N.J., Coyne, J. and Duvall, J., 'Adopted and biological children in the clinic: family, parental and child characteristics', *Journal of Child Psychology and Psychiat*ry, Vol. 34, No. 4., 1993, pp. 545-62.

44 Cadoret, R.J., *et al*., 'Early life psycho-social events and adult affective symptoms', in Robins, and Rutter, *Straight and Devious Pathways from Childhood to Adolescence, op. cit*.; see also Brandon, S., Holland, A. and Murray, R., 'The genetics of schizophrenia and its implications', *Adoption and Fostering*, Vol. 9, No. 2, 1985, pp. 39-45.

45 Rowe, J. and Lambert, L., *Children Who Wait*, London: Association of British Adoption Agencies, 1973.

46 Triseliotis and Russell, *Hard to Place, op. cit.*

47 Bentavim, A. and Gilmour, L., 'A family therapy inter-actional approach to decision making in childcare, access and custody cases', *Journal of Family Therapy*, Vol. 3, 1981, pp. 65-77.

48 Tizard, B., *Adoption: A Second Chance*, London: Open Books, 1977.

49 Jacka, A.A., *Adoption in Brief*, Slough: National Foundation for Educational Research, 1973.

50 Hill, M. and Triseliotis, J., 'The transition from long-term care to adoption', in Hudson, J. and Galaway, B., *The State as Parent*, London: Kluwer Academic Press, 1989, p. 102.

51 Triseliotis and Russell, *Hard to Place*, *op. cit.*, p. 137.

52 *Ibid.*, p. 181.

53 Triseliotis and Russell (p. 147) are referring to Miller, E.J and Gwynne, G.V., *A Life Apart,* London: Tavistock, 1972: 'the lack of any actual or potential role that confers a positive status in the wider society is tantamount to being socially dead'. The foremost work on institutions is that of Goodman, E., *Asylums: Essays on the Social Situation of Mental Patients and Other Inmates*, New York: Doubleday Anchor Books, 1961.

54 Mallows, M., 'Trans-racial Adoption: the most open adoption' in Mullender, A. (ed.), *Open Adoption*, London: British Agencies for Adoption and Fostering, 1991, p. 82.

55 In 1979, a survey of social services departments showed that in some areas as many as 50 per cent of children in care were already from these groups. Lindsay-Smith, C., 'Black children who wait', *Adoption and Fostering,* No.1, 1979.

56 Leigh Chambers from British Agencies for Adoption Fostering quoted by Carlisle, D., in 'Tugging at heart strings', in *Community Care*, 14-20 November 1996, p. 11.

57 Simon, R.J., 'Adoption of black children by white parents in the USA', in Bean, P., *Adoption: Essays in Social Policy, Law and Sociology*, London: Tavistock, 1984, p. 232.

58 See summary of research in Thoburn, J., *Success and Failure in Permanent Family Placement*, Aldershot: Avebury, 1990, p. 57.

59 Zastrow, C.H., *Outcome of Black Children—White Parents Trans-racial Adoptions*, San Francisco: R.&.E Research Associates, inc., 1997. See also Kadushin, A., *Child Welfare Services*, New York: Macmillan, 1972.

60 Grow, L. and Shapiro, D., 'Adoption of black children by white parents', *Child Welfare,* January 1975.

61 For example: One such in Britain was C. Bagley and L. Young's involving 51 trans-racial adoptions. One to four years after the placement, 94 per cent of the children and 75 per cent of the adoptive parents were assessed as having made a good or satisfactory adjustment to their changed family status. Forty-four of the 51 sets of parents were interviewed when the children were aged 12 to 16, when 83 per cent of the trans-racial placements were assessed as a success. ['The identity, adjustment and achievement of trans-racially adopted children: a review and empirical report', in Verma, G. and Bagley, L. (eds.), *Race, Education and Identity*, London: Macmillan, 1979.] Also see; Shireman, J. and Johnson, P., 'A longitudinal study of black adoptions', *Social Work*, May-June 1986. This study of 118 black children placed for adoption when under the age of three, with black or white parents, followed-up at four and eight. No placements were disrupted. On the basis of standardised tests, parents' reports and researchers observations, the adjustment of 56 of the 71 who agreed to take part was rated as excellent or good, at 79 per cent.

62 Gill, D. and Jackson, B., *Adoption and Race*, London: Batsford, 1983.

63 Tizard, B., *Adoption: A Second Chance*, London: Open Books, 1977, p. 185.

64 Day, D., *The Adoption of Black Children*, Lexington: Lexington Books, 1979; also see Simon, R.J., 'Adoption of black children by white parents in the USA', in Bean, P. (ed.), *Adoption: Essays in Social Policy, Law, and Sociology*, London: Tavistock, 1984.

65 Bagley and Young, 'The identity, adjustment and achievement of trans-racially adopted children: a review and empirical report', *op. cit.*

66 Simon, R.J., 'An assessment of racial awareness, preference and self-identity among white and adopted non-white children', *Social Problems*, October 1974; also Simon, R.J. and Altstein, H., *Trans-racial Adoption*, New York: John Wiley & Sons, 1977.

67 Simon, 'Adoption of black children by white parents in the USA', *op. cit.*, p. 238.

68 Simon, R.J. and Alstein, H., *Trans-racial Adoption: A Follow-Up*, Lexington: Lexington Books, 1981.

69 Simon, 'Adoption of black children by white parents in the USA', *op. cit.*, p. 239.

70 *Ibid.*, p. 240.

71 Hodges, J. and Tizard, B., letter to the Editor, *New Society*, 14 July 1983.

72 Thoburn, J., *Review of Research Relating to Adoption*, Inter-departmental review of adoption law: background paper No 2, Department of Health, 1990, p. 55.

73 Dale, D., *Denying Homes to Black Children*, London: Social Affairs Unit, Research Report No. 8, undated, p. 32.

74 Kudashin, A., *Adopting Older Children*, New York: Columbia University Press, 1970, p. 224.

75 Heath, A., Colton, M. and Aldgate, J., 'Failure to escape: a longitudinal study of foster children's educational attainment', *British Journal of Social Work*, Vol. 24, 1989, pp. 241-60.

76 Garnett, L., *Leaving Care and After*, London: National Children's Bureau 1992; and Stein, M. and Carey, K., *Leaving Care*, Oxford: Blackwell, 1986.

77 Prison Reform Trust, *The Identikit Prisoner*, 1991; see also the National Prison Survey, Home Office, 1991.

78 '"One of the major residential placements for kids who age out of the system is jail", says Nancy Nazaroff, clinical director at Project Rap, in Beverly, which deals with homeless youths. "In jail, they're warm, they get food and a roof over their head, they can get education and substance abuse help, and there's TV." Some girls have a different career strategy: early pregnancy. Then they can get a monthly welfare check, food stamps, Medicaid, and even day care.' [English, B., 'Nobody's children: too old for foster care, too young for independence', *The Boston Globe,* 16 October 1994, p. 39.]

79 Rosen, A.C., 'The social and emotional development of children in long-term residential care', *Therapeutic Education*, Spring 1971.

80 Rutter, Quinton and Hill, 'Adult outcome of institution-reared children: males and females compared', *op. cit.*

81 Rowe and Lambert, *Children Who Wait, op. cit.*, pp. 114-15.

82 Utting, W., *People Like Us: The Report of the Review of the Safeguards for Children Living Away from Home*, Department of Health and Welsh Office, 1997, pp. 1-3; see also Taylor, A., 'Hostages to fortune: the abuse of children in care', unpublished paper, 1996.

83 Widespread abuse is also alleged for South Glamorgan, where Geoffrey Morris was jailed for indecent assaults against teenage boys. Another worker committed suicide and a third man has been convicted of offences elsewhere.

84 Bunyan N., 'Boys abused on "unimaginable scale" in home', *The Daily Telegraph*, 23 January 1997.

85 The boys are described as being '...neglected, ill-fed and clothed, dirty and often infested, and little attention was paid to signs of distress or addiction to solvents. Bryn Estyn seemed little better than a human warehouse, dominated by a malaise and unease which probably arose from the conflict between fickle conscience and failure to act'. [Taylor, 'Hostages to fortune: the abuse of children in care', *op. cit.*]

86 Alan Langshaw, care worker, pleaded guilty to 30 counts of serious sexual assaults and indecent assaults against boys aged under 16 at homes in Cheshire and Liverpool. Jailed for ten years.

Colin Dick, care worker, guilty of nine serious sexual offences and indecent assaults against children at one home in Cheshire. Jailed for four years.

Dennis Grain, care worker, pleaded guilty to 19 cases of serious sexual offences and indecent assault at homes in Cheshire and Yorkshire. Jailed for seven years.

Terrence Hoskin, guilty of 22 counts of indecent assault and physical assault and serious sexual offences at home where he was head. Jailed for eight years.

John Clarke, convicted of indecent and physical assault at a care home in Cheshire. Jailed for three and a half years.

Roy Shuttleworth, care worker, found guilty of 11 counts of serious sexual offences and indecent assaults on boys in a care home in Cheshire. Jailed for 10 years.

John Clarke, convicted of five indecent assaults at children's homes. Jailed for three and a half years.

James Traynor, convicted of five indecent assaults and one serious sexual assault. Jailed for eight years.

Keith Laverack, convicted of 20 serious sexual assaults and indecent assaults. Jailed for 18 years.

In turn, two men (Philip Savage and Edward Stanton) have been respectively jailed for 13 and 15 years in Liverpool in prosecutions arising from the Cheshire inquiry

87 Report 'The Hackney scandal', *Evening Standard*, 4 September 1996.

88 Utting, *People Like Us: The Report of the Review of the Safeguards for Children Living Away from Home*, *op. cit*.

89 A 20-year-old is suing Durham Council, the Aycliffe Centre and five individuals for personal injuries. Claiming that he worked as a rent boy at 14, and that those looking after him failed in their duty of care, Carl August maintains that he was '...systematically abused for three years and allowed to visit the gay scene'. ['Aycliffe at centre of new abuse allegations', *Community Care*, 14-20 November 1996.]

90 Survey of clients, APA Community Drug and Alcohol Initiatives, London, 1996.

91 *Children in the Public Care: A Review of Residential Childcare*, London: HMSO, 1991.

92 *Ibid*., p. 26.

93 Barth, R.P., Courtney, M., Berrick, J.D. and Albert, V., *From Child Abuse to Permanency Planning*, New York: Aldine de Gruyter, 1994, p. 258.

94 Murch, M. and Thorpe, Rt. Hon. Lord Justice, 'The development of the family justice system in England and Wales: past, present, and future', in Salgo, L. (ed.), *The Family Justice System*, Collegium Budapest Workshop, Series No. 3, 1997, pp. 3-34.

95 See *Agreement and Freeing*, Discussion Paper Number 2 Inter-Departmental Review of Adoption Law, Department of Health, September 1991.

96 Murch, M. Lowe, N., Borkowski, M., Copner, R. and Griew, K., *Pathways to Adoption*, Research Project Socio-Legal Centre for Family Studies, University of Bristol, London: HMSO, 1993.

97 *Ibid.*, pp. 243-44.

98 *For Children's Sake: An SSI Inspection of Local Authority Adoption Services*, Social Services Inspectorate, *op. cit.*

99 There is also, of course, the question of whether child welfare services should be disaggregated and turned over to non-profit agencies. Kansas has become the first state in the USA to privatise its adoption, foster care, and family preservation services. Contractors must agree to serve each child for a fixed price, with incentives to work intensively with the parents to get the child back home or, if that is not possible, to proceed to the termination of parental rights. Competition has encouraged providers to create an array of partnerships and consortia to address their weaknesses. [Eggers, W.D., 'There's no place like home', *Policy Review*, May - June 1997, pp. 43-47.]

Felicity Collier

1 Morgan, P., *Adoption and the Care of Children: The British and American Experience*, London: IEA, 1998, p. 66.

2 Fergusson, D.M., Lynskey, M. and Horwood, J.L., 'The adolescent outcomes of adoption: a 16-year longitudinal study', *The Journal of Child Psychology and Psychiatry*, Vol. 36, No. 4, May 1995, pp. 597-615.

3 Jardine, S., 'Transracial placements: an adoptee's perspective', in Barn, R. (ed.),*Working With Black Children and Adolescents In Need* London: British Agencies for Adoption and Fostering, 1999, p. 148.

4 House of Commons Select Committee, *Children Looked After by Local Authorities*, Health Committee Second Report, Vol. 1, July 1998.

5 'Stephen Lawrence Inquiry', Report of an inquiry by Sir William MacPherson of Cluny, London: HMSO, 1999.

6 Hayes, M., 'Transracial adopted people's support group', chapter 21 in Phillips, R. and McWilliam, E. (eds.), *After Adoption: Working with Adoptive Families*, London: British Agencies for Adoption and Fostering, 1996, p. 186.

7 Ince, L., *Making It Alone: A Study of the Care Experiences of Young Black People*, London: British Agencies for Adoption and Fostering, 1998, ch. 7, pp. 49-86.

8 Morgan, *Adoption and the Care of Children, op. cit.*, p. 114.

9 *Ibid.*, p. 114.

10 Owen, M., *Novices, Old Hands and Professionals: Adoption by Single People*, London: British Agencies for Adoption and Fostering, 1999, p. 183.

11 Ivaldi, G., *Children Adopted from Care: An Examination of Agency Adoptions in England 1996*, London: British Agencies for Adoption and Fostering, 1998.

12 Collier, F., *Action Plan to Improve Adoption Services*, London: British Agencies for Adoption and Fostering, 1998. For free copies of the Action Plan please contact BAAF on 0171 593 2011.

Jim Richards

1 Morgan, P., *Who Needs Parents?* London: IEA, 1996.

2 *Adoption: Achieving the Right Balance*, LAC (98) 20, HMSO: Department of Health, 1998.

3 *For Children's Sake: An SSI Inspection of Local Authority Adoption Services Social Services*, Social Services Inspectorate, Department of Health, 1996; *Meeting the Challenges of Changes in Adoption: Inspection of Voluntary Adoption Agencies*, Social Services Inspectorate, Department of Health, 1999; *Modern Social Services: A Commitment to Improve*, the 8th Annual Report of the Chief Inspector of Social Services, Department of Health, 1999.

4 Holman, B., *Child Care Revisited: The Children's Departments 1948-1971*, London: Institute of Childcare and Social Education, 1998.

5 Morgan, P., *Adoption and the Care of Children: The British and American Experience*, London: IEA, 1998.

6 *SSI Inspection of Local Authority Fostering 1995-96: National Summary Report*. Department of Health, 1996.

7 *For Children's Sake, op. cit.*, p. 124.

8 *For Children's Sake, op. cit.* pp. 42-43.

9 *Children Looked After by Local Authorities: Year Ending 31 March 1998, England*, Department of Health, 1999.

10 Ivaldi, G., *Children Adopted from Care: An Examination of Agency Adoptions in England 1996*, London: British Agencies for Adoption and Fostering, 1998.

11 *Adoption: Achieving the Right Balance*, *op. cit.*

12 Holman, *Child Care Revisited, op. cit.*

13 Lowe, N., Murch, M. *et al.*, *Supporting Adoption: Reframing the Approach*, London: British Agencies for Adoption and Fostering, 1999.

14 Thorpe, D., *Evaluating Child Protection*, Open University Press,1994.

Barbara Ballis Lal

1 Simon, R. and Altstein, H., *Transracial Adoption*, New York: Wiley, 1977; Simon, R., Altstein, H. and Melli, M., *The Case For Trans-racial Adoption*, Washington DC: American University Press, 1994; Bartholet, E., 'Where do black children belong? The politics of race matching in adoption', *Pennsylvania Law Review*, Vol. 139, 1991, pp. 1163, 1198-99. Bartholet, E., *Family Bonds, Adoption and the Politics of Parenting*, New York: Houghton Mifflin, 1993; Hayes, P., 'Transracial adoption: politics and ideology', Child Welfare, Vol. LXXII, No. 3, May-June, 1993, pp. 301-10. Hayes, P., 'The ideological attack on transracial adoption in the USA and Britain', International Journal of Law and Family, Vol. 9, 1995, pp. 1-22; Silverman, A.R., 'Outcomes of transracial adoption', in *The Future of Children*, special issue on adoption, Centre for the Future of Children, Vol. 3, No. 1, Spring 1993; pp. 104-118.

2 Rhodes, P., 'The emergence of a new policy: racial matching in fostering and adoption', *New Community*, Vol. 18, No. 2, 1992, pp. 191-208.

3 'Race' and 'ethnicity' are social constructions, that is to say, these are ways of thinking about and differentiating between individuals and groups which are influenced by the categories available to us, for example, through language or history and convention. Accordingly, what people mean by race and ethnicity, as well as the salience of these categories, changes over time and varies between groups and contexts. In this essay, I refer to conventional meanings and use the term 'race' to stand for physical characteristics, and especially colour, and

ethnicity to stand for culture of origin and/or residence. These categories sometimes are intended to overlap, as for example, in the designations African-American and non-white Hispanic used in many USA studies or 'Black-Caribbean' and 'Black-Other' used in the British Census, 1991. (Consider what is intended to be conveyed by the designations 'British-born Afro-Caribbean' or Jews-at various times thought to be both race and ethnic group .) For a more extensive discussion of the categories of race and ethnicity which differs from my own point of view, see Cornell, S. and Hartmann, D., *Ethnicity and Race*, Thousand Oaks: Pine Forge Press, 1998.

4 Morgan, P., *Adoption and the Care of Children*, London: IEA, 1998, pp. 105-14. Additional studies include Grow, L. and Shapiro, D., *Black Children, White Parents*, New York: Child Welfare League of America, 1974; Dale, D., *The Adoption of Black Children: Counteracting Institutional Discrimination*, Lexington MA: Lexington Books, 1979; Kim, S. and Kim, B.S., 'Adoption of Korean children by New York area couples', *Child Welfare*, Vol. 5, 1979, pp. 419-27; Richards, B., 'Family, Race and Identity', *Adoption and Fostering*, Vol. 14, No. 2, 1987, pp. 10-13; Tizard, B. and Phoenix, A., 'Black identity and trans-racial adoption', in *New Community*, Vol. 15, No. 3, 1989, pp. 427-37; Silverman, A.R. and Feigelman, W., 'Adjustment in interracial adopteęs: an overview', in Brodzinsky, D. and Schechter, M.D., *The Psychology of Adoption*, Oxford: Oxford University Press, 1990; Tizard, B., 'Inter-country adoption: a review of the evidence', *Journal of Child Psychology and Psychiatry*, Vol. 32, No. 7, 1990, pp. 43-56; Bagley, C., 1993 'Trans-racial adoption in Britain: a follow-up study with policy considerations', *Child Welfare*, Vol. 43, No. 3, 1993, pp. 285-99; *The Future of Children*, special issue on adoption, *op. cit.*; Lythcott-Haimes, J., 'Where do mixed babies belong? Racial classification in America and its implications for trans-racial adoption', *Harvard Civil Rights-Civil Liberties Law Review*, Vol. 29, 1994, pp. 531-58; O'Brien, C., 'Trans-racial adoption in Hong Kong', *Child Welfare*,Vol. 73, No. 4, 1994, pp. 319-29; Simon, Altstein and Melli, *The Case For Trans-racial Adoption*, *op. cit.*; Griffith, E., 'Forensic and policy implications of the trans-racial adoption debate', *Bulletin of the American Academy of Psychiatric Law*, Vol. 23, No. 4, 1995, pp. 501-11; Rahdert, M., 'Trans-racial adoption: a constitutional perspective', *Temple Law Review*, Vol 68, 1995,

pp. 1687-1714; Gabor, I. and Aldridge, J. (eds.), *In the Best Interests of the Child, Culture, Identity and Trans-racial Adoption*, 1996, London: Free Association Books; Vroegh, K. 'Trans-racial adoptees: developmental status after 17 years', American Orthopsychiatric Association, Vol. 67 No. 4, 1997, pp. 568-75. Feigelman, W. and Silverman, A.R., *Chosen Children*, New York: Prager, 1983. This list is not exhaustive.

5 Morgan reviews these studies throughout her book.

6 The Multiethnic Placement Act, 1994, P.L. 103-382 S553, Stat. 405. 103 Congress, 2nd. Session, H.R. 4181. Two years later the Inter-Ethnic Adoption Provisions attached to the Small Business Job Protection Act further limited the scope for using race, ethnicity or national origin as a deterrent to foster or adoption placements. US Department of Health and Human Services, Small Business Job Protection Act, Inter-Ethnic Adoption Provisions, 1996.

7 Hirst, J., 'When love is not all you need', *Community Care*, 11-17 June 1998, pp. 8-9.

8 Two such advocacy groups are The Adoption Forum and the Campaign for Inter-country Adoption.

9 Hague Conference on Private International Law 1992, 'Report on inter-country adoption', Preliminary Document No. 1, drawn up by J.H.A. van Loon (1990).

10 Small, J., 'The crisis in adoption', *The International Journal of Social Psychiatry*, Vol. 30, 1984, pp. 129-42; Small, J., 'Trans-racial placements: conflicts and contradictions', in Cheetham, A. and Small, J. (eds.), *Social Work with Black Children and Their Families*, London: Batsford, 1986; Giles, T. and Kroll, J., *Barriers to Same Race Placement*, St. Paul, MN: North American Council on Adoptable Children, 1991; Gould, K.H., 1991 'Limiting damage is not enough: a minority perspective on child welfare issues', in Everett, J.E. *et al.* (eds.), *Child Welfare: An Africentric Perspective*, New Brunswick, NJ: Rutgers University Press, 1991, pp. 58-77; McRoy, R.G., 'Attachment and racial identity issues: implications for child placement making decisions', *Journal of Multicultural Social Work*, Vol. 3, 1994, pp. 59-74; Hollingsworth, L.D., 'Promoting same race adoption for children of color', *Social Work*, Vol. 43, No. 2, 1998, pp. 97-116; Thoburn, J., Norford, L.,Rashid, S.P., *Permanent Family Placement For Children of Minority Ethnic Origin*, Norwich: Centre for Research on the Child and

Family, University of East Anglia, 1998.

Other studies not cited by Morgan include Chestang, L., 'The dilemma of biracial adoption', *Social Work*, Vol. 17, No. 3, 1972, pp. 100-05; Chimezie, A., 'Bold but irrelevant: Grow and Shapiro on trans-racial adoption', *Child Welfare*, Vol. 56, No. 2, 1977, pp. 75-86; McRoy, R. and Zurcher, L., *Transracial and Inracial Adoptees: The Adolescent Years*, Springfield Ill: Charles C. Thomas,1983; Flechman-Smith, B., 'Effects of race on adoption and fostering', *International Journal of Social Psychiatry*, Vol. 30, No. 1-2, 1984, pp. 121-28; Small, J., 'New black families', *Adoption and Fostering*, Vol. 6, No. 3, 1982, pp. 35-39; Perry, T., 'Race and child placement: the best interest test and the cost of discretion', *Journal of Family Law*, Vol. 29, p. 51; Folaron,G., 'Placement considerations for children of mixed African-American and caucasian parentage', *Child Welfare*, Vol. 72, No. 2, 1993, pp. 113-25. This list is not exhaustive.

11 Carp, E.W., *Family Matters: Secrecy and Disclosure in the History of Adoption*, Cambridge: Harvard University Press, 1998, quoted in Elshtain, J.B., 'The chosen family', *The New Republic*, September14&21 1998, pp. 45-53.

12 As Julius Lester, a leading member of the Southern Student Organizing Committee, pointed out in 1966: 'At one time black people desperately wanted to be American, to communicate with whites, to live in the Beloved Community. Now that is irrelevant. They know that it can't be until whites want it to be and it is obvious now that whites don't want it', in Lester, J. 'The angry children of Malcolm X', Nashville Tenn: Southern Student Organizing Committee, 1966, Vol. 9. Among the numerous discussions on this topic see, Carmichael, S. and Hamilton, C.V., *Black Power: The Politics of Liberation in America*, New York: Vintage Books, 1992; Farley, R., *The New American Reality*, New York: Russell Sage, 1996; Lal, B.B., 'Charting a course in a "new" American landscape: theories of ethnicity after 1965', *Indian Journal of Gender Studies*, Vol. 4, 1997, pp. 261-68; Macedo, S. (ed.), *Reassessing the Sixties: Debating the Political and Cultural Legacy*, London: W.W. Norton and Company, 1997.

13 For a useful discussion of collective identity see Calhoun, C., 'Social theory and the politics of identity', in Calhoun, C. (ed.), *Social Theory and the Politics of Identity*, Oxford: Blackwell, 1994, pp 9-36.

14 For further discussion of an essentialist model of identity see Lal, B.B., 'Symbolic interaction theories', in *American Behavioral Scientist*, Special Issue, 38, January 1995, pp. 421-41; Lal, B.B., 'Ethnic identity entrepreneurs: their role in transracial and intercountry adoptions', *Asian and Pacific Migration Journal*, Vol. 6, No. 3-4, 1997, pp. 385-413. For a discussion of rights, needs and the 'psychiatric presentation of a political agenda' by opponents of same-race placements which complements the idea of identity deficits see, Hayes, 'Transracial adoption: politics and ideology', *op. cit.* and Hayes, 'The ideological attack on transracial adoption in the USA and Britain', *op. cit.* While my approach to the discussion of identity in the debate about trans-racial and inter-country adoptions is a reflection of my commitment both to particular sociological perspectives, namely,, symbolic interactionism and those of Max Weber and Frank Parkin, as well as the study of the history of theories of ethnicity in the USA and Britain, I agree with many of Hayes' conclusions.

15 Steinberg, S., *The Ethnic Myth*, Boston: Beacon Press, 1981; Kauffman, L.A., 'The anti-politics of identity', *Socialist Review*, Vol. 20, No. 1, 1990, pp. 67-80; Gitlin, T., 'Fragmentation of the idea of the Left', in Calhoun, 'Social Theory and the Politics of Identity', *op. cit.*, pp. 150-174.

16 For example, see Ecoles, A., *Daring to be Bad: Radical Feminism in America 1967-1975*, Minneapolis: University of Minnisota Press, 1989.

17 Wilson, J.W., *The Declining Significance of Race: Blacks and Changing American Institutions*, Chicago: University of Chicago Press, 1978; Wilson, J.W., *The Truly Disadvantaged: The Inner City, The Underclass and Public Policy*, Chicago: University of Chicago Press, 1987; Wilson, J., *When Work Disappears*, Chicago: University of Chicago Press, 1996.

18 Tizard and Phoenix, 'Black identity and trans-racial adoption', *op. cit.*; Tizard, B. and Phoenix, A., *Black, White Or Mixed Race?*, New York: Routledge, 1993; Back, L., 'Social context and racist name calling: an ethnographic perspective on racist talk within a South London adolescent community', *The European Journal of Intercultural Studies*, Vol. 1, No. 3, 1991, pp. 19-38; Back, L., *New Ethnicities and Urban Culture*, London: UCL Press, 1996; Ballard, R. and Kalra, V.S., *The Ethnic Dimensions of The 1991 Census*, Manchester: The University of Manchester, 1994.

Tariq Modood has been a constant critic of the tendency to overlook significant differences, such as that of religion, among non-white groups in Britain. In collapsing the distinction between race and culture, the difference between colour-racism and cultural-racism is obscured. Modood, T., '"Black", Racial Equality and Asian Identity', *New Community*, XIV, Spring 1988, pp. 397-404; Modood, T., *Not Easy Being British*, Stoke-on Trent: Runnymede Trust and Trentham Books, 1992; Modood, T., Beishon, S. and Virdee, S., *Changing Ethnic Identities*, London: Policy Studies Institute, 1994. Ironically, most recently colour-blindness has been cited as a new form of racism because this approach overlooks the significance and meaning of being a person of colour. For example, see Carr, L., *'Color-Blind' Racism*, Thousand Oaks: Sage, 1998. Also, see Nieto, S., *Affirming Diversity: The Sociopolitical Context of Multicultural Education*, New York: Longman, 1992. S., *Changing Ethnic Identities*, London: Policy Studies Institute, 1994.

19 Jacoby, R., 'The myth of multiculturalism', in *The New Left Review*, Vol. 208, November 1994, pp. 121-27; Gans, H., 'Symbolic ethnicity', reprinted in Sollors, S. (ed.), *Theories of Ethnicity, A Classical Reader*, New York: New York University Press, 1979, pp. 425-59; McAdoo, H.P., *Black Families*, Thousand Oaks: Sage, 1997.

20 National Association of Black Social Workers, 'Position paper on transracial adoption' (1978), cited in Cheetham, J., (ed.), 'Introduction to the Issues', *Social Work and Ethnicity*, London: George Allen & Unwin, 1982, pp. 3-19.

21 National Association of Black Social Workers, 'Preserving African American Families', Position Statement, Detroit, 1994.

22 National Association of Social Workers, 'Social work speaks: NASW policy statements', 4th edition, Washington DC: NASW Press, 1997.

23 British Agencies for Adoption and Fostering, 'Practice Note 13: The Placement Needs of Black Children', London, 1987.

24 British Agencies for Adoption and Fostering, 'Inter-country adoption, information and guidance, London, 1998, p. 4.

25 See Morgan, and citations above and endnote 10.

26 BAAF, 'Inter-country adoption, information and guidance, *op. cit*. p. 4.

27 Bartholet, 'International Adoption' *op. cit*., pp. 95-99;Bartholet, E., 'International adoption: proriety, prospects and pragmatics, *Journal of the American Academy of Matrimonial Lawyers*, Vol. 13, No. 2, Winter 1996, pp. 181-210; Scanlon, T., Tomkins, A., Lynch, M. and Scanlon, F., 'Street children in Latin America', *British Medical Journal*, Vol. 316, No. 7144, 23 May 1998.

28 '6.3 Brides for Seven Brothers', *The Economist*, 19 December 1998, pp. 56-58; Johnson, K., Banghan, H. and Liyao, W., 'Infant abandonment and adoption in China', *Population and Development Review*, Vol. 24, No. 3, 1998, pp. 469-503.

29 For children sources of identity based upon association outside the family, biological or adopted, include neighborhood, school, clubs such as those organised around drama, music, chess, religion, and community service, athletic teams, and friendship groups. The categories of consent and descent are discussed by Sollors, W., *Beyond Ethnicity: Consent and Descent in American Culture*, New York: Oxford University Press, 1986.

30 Lal, 'Symbolic interaction theories', *op. cit*. See also Wallman, S., 'Introduction: the scope for ethnicity', in *Ethnicity At Work*, London: Macmillan, 1979, pp. ix-xii and pp.1-14; Wallman, S., 'Identity options', in Fried, C. (ed.), *Minorities: Community and Identity*, Berlin, New York: Springer-Verlag, 1983, pp. 69-78. Patterson, O., 'Context and choice in ethnic allegiance', in Glazer, N. and Moynihan, D. (eds.), *Ethnicity, Theory and Experience*, Cambridge, MA: Harvard University Press, 1975, 305-49; Gans, 'Symbolic ethnicity', *op. cit*.; Phoenix, 'Black identity and trans-racial adoption', *op. cit*. However, Waters emphasises that choice is much more limited for people of colour, see Waters, M.S., *Ethnic Options*, Los Angeles: University of California Press, 1990.

31 Spickard, P.R., *Mixed Blood: Intermarriage and Ethnic Identity in Twentieth Century America*, Madison: University of Wisconsin Press, 1989; Root, M.P. (ed.), *Racially Mixed People In America*, London: Sage, 1992; Root, M.P. (ed.), *The Multiracial Experience*, London: Sage, 1996; Tizard and Phoenix, *Black, White Or Mixed Race?*, *op. cit*.

32 Ogbu, J., *Minority Education and Caste: The American System in Cross-Cultural Perspective*, New York: Academic Press, 1978; Portes, A. and Zhou, M., 'The new second generation: segmented assimilation and its variants among post-1965 immigrant youth', *Annals, American Academy of Political Science*, Vol. 530, 1993, pp. 74-98; Zhou, M., 'Growing up American: the challenge confronting immigrant children and children of immigrants', in *Annual Review of Sociology*, Vol. 23, 1997, pp. 63-95; Zhou, M., Bankston, C., *Growing Up American: How Vietnamese Children Adapt to Life in the United States*, New York: Russell Sage Foundation, 1998; Werbner, P. and Modood, T. (eds.), *Debating Cultural Hybridity, Multi-Cultural Identities and the Politics of Anti-Racism*, London: Zed Books, 1997.

33 Brodzinsky, D. and Schechter, M.D., *The Psychology of Adoption*, New York and Oxford: Oxford University Press, 1990; Adoption issue, *The Future of Children*, *op. cit.*

34 Lal, 'Ethnic identity entrepreneurs' *op. cit.*.

35 Gossett, T., *Race: The History of an Idea in America*, New York: Schocken Books, 19965; Takaki, R., 'Reflections on racial patterns in America', in Takaki, R. (ed.), *From Different Shores: Perspectives on Race and Ethnicity in America*, Oxford: Oxford University Press, 1994.

36 Social closure is a 'process by which social collectivities seek to maximize rewards by restricting access to resources and opportunities to a limited circle of eligibles' on the basis of 'singling out of certain social or physical attributes as the justificatory basis of exclusion', Parkin, F., 'Marxism and class theory: a bourgeois critique', (1979) reprinted in Grusky, D. (ed.), *Social Stratification in Sociological Perspective*, Boulder: Westview Press, 1994, p. 143. What is 'seized upon' is arbitrary as long as it can be utilized to monopolize opportunities, in particular, economic opportunities. Unlike those recruited from the dominant group, ethnic identity entrepreneurs representing subordinated/minority groups do not usually create the context in which their services are required but instead respond to structurally generated and unacceptable inequalities in the distribution of scarce resources, such as wealth, income and status and limited accessibility to valued experience, such as interesting, well-paid occupations and higher education.

37 Goffman, E., 'The interaction order', in *American Sociological Review*, Vol. 48, February 1983, pp. 1-17.

38 Looking at figures for 1995 in the USA gives us some idea of the magnitude of the difference between the number of children in care and those available for adoption. Of the 483,629 children in foster care at the end of 1995, approximately 74,931 had a goal of adoption, but were not yet legally free for adoption. An additional 32,236 were legally free and waiting adoption of which 50 per cent were African American and 97 per cent were older that one year of age. 'Adoption Fact Sheet', Washington, DC: Child Welfare League of America, 1997. These figures can be usefully compared to those cited by Morgan, as well as those presented by *The Future of Children*, Adoption issue, *op. cit*.

Conna Craig

1 McNamara, E. , 'Two-tier justice hurts children', *Boston Sunday Globe*, 14 February 1999.

2 Morgan, P., *Adoption and the Care of Children: The British and American Experience*, London: IEA, 1998, p. 45.

3 *Ibid.* , pp. 129-30.

4 Wong, D.S., 'Tighter rules set for foster parents', *Boston Globe*, 26 September 1998, p. 1.

Chris Hanvey

1 Chancellor of the Exchequer, Budget Speech, 2 July,1997.

2 Morgan, P., *Adoption and the Care of Children: The British and American Experience*, London: IEA, 1998.

3 *Report of the Committee of Inquiry into the Care and Supervision Provided in Relation to Maria Colwell*, London: HMSO, 1974.

4 Morgan, *op. cit.*, p. 4.

5 *Barnardos Press Release*, 8 December 1997.

6 Utting, W., *People Like Us: The Report of the Review of the Safeguards for Children Living Away from Home*, Department of Health and Welsh Office, 1997, Summary Report, p. 7.

7 Morgan, *op. cit.*, p. 154.

8 CIPFA evidence to *Childhood Matters: Report of the National Commission of Inquiry into the Prevention of Childhood Abuse*, Vol. 2, London: NSPCC, 1996, Appendix 7, pp. 181, 214-18.

9 *Quality Protects*, Department of Health, London: 1998.

10 Hodgkin, R. and Newell, P., *Effective Government Structures for Children: Report of a Gulbenkian Foundation Inquiry*, London: Calouste Gulbenkian Foundation, 1996.

Karen Irving

1 Ivaldi, G., *Children Adopted From Care: An Examination of Agency Adoptions in England, 1996*, Key Findings, British Agencies for Adoption and Fostering Adoption Statistics Project, 1998.

2 Rowe, J. and Lambert, L., *Children Who Wait*, London: Association of British Adoption Agencies, 1973.

3 Ivaldi, *Children Adopted From Care, op. cit.*, p. 4.

4 *Ibid.*, p. 6.

5 Kirton, D., 'A very blinkered view', review in *Adoption & Fostering* Vol. 22, No. 2, Summer 1998.

Liv O'Hanlon

1 Humphreys, M., *Empty Cradles*, London: Doubleday, 1994. The Child Migrant Trust charity has been established to help those involved.

2 Department of Health, *Children Looked After by Local Authorities: Year Ending 31 March 1998, England*, Government Statistical Service, 1999.

3 *Ibid*, p. 13.

4 Tizard, B., *Adoption: A Second Chance*, London: Open Books, 1977.

5 Ivaldi, G., *Children Adopted From Care: An Examination of Agency Adoptions in England, 1996*, London: British Agencies for Adoption and Fostering Adoption, 1998.

6 If you would like a copy of The Adoption Forum's paper proposing the establishment of an independent central authority, please contact Liz Siefers, Secretary, The Adoption Forum on 01737 357279.

Richard Whitfield

1 House of Commons Health Select Committee, *Children Looked After by Local Authorities*, London: HMSO, 1998.

2 Audit Commission, *Local Authority Performance Indicators: Services for People with Special Needs in England*, London: Audit Commission Publications,1999.

3 Department of Health, *Quality Protects*, London: HMSO, 1998.

4 Morgan, P., *Adoption and the Care of Children: the British and American Experience*, London: IEA, 1998.

5 Adapted and extended from: Fagan, P.F., *Why Serious Welfare Reform Must Include Serious Adoption Reform*, Washington DC: Heritage Foundation, 1996.

6 Leader, *The Times*, 19 January 1999.

7 Whitfield, R., 'Taking our children seriously: core values for teachers and parents', chapter 12, in David, K. and Charlton, T. (eds.), *Pastoral Care Matters in Middle and Primary Schools*, London: Routledge, 1996.

8 See, for example: Gardner, H., *Multiple Intelligences: The Theory in Practice*, New York: Basic Books, 1993; Goleman, D., *Emotional Intelligence*, New York: Bantam, 1995.

9 Crandell, L.E. and Hobson, R.P., 'Individual differences in young children's IQ: a social-developmental perspective', *Journal of Child Psychology and Psychiatry*, Vol. 40, No. 3, 1999, pp. 455-64.

10 See, for example: Atkinson, L. and Zucker, K.J. (eds.), *Attachment and Psychopathology*, New York: Guildford Press, 1997; Bowlby J.A., *Secure Base: Clinical Applications of Attachment Theory*, London: Routledge, 1988; Holmes, J., *John Bowlby and Attachment Theory*, London: Routledge, 1993; Howe, D., *Patterns of Adoption: Nature, Nurture and Psychosocial Development*, Oxford: Blackwell, 1998 (this book helpfully links cases of adoption to categories of attachment); Kraemer, S. and Roberts, J., *The Politics of Attachment: Towards a Secure Society*, London: Free Association Books, 1996.

11 For a general introduction, see Greenfield, S., *The Human Brain: A Guided Tour*, London: Weidenfield and Nicholson, 1997.

12 Morgan, *Adoption and the Care of Children, op. cit.*

13 Maughan, B., Collishaw, S. and Pickles, A., 'School achievement and adult qualifications among adoptees: a longitudinal study', *Journal of Child Psychology and Psychiatry*, Vol. 39, No. 5, 1998, pp. 669-85.

14 Rutter, M. and Study Team, 'Developmental catch-up, and deficit, following adoption after severe early privation', *Journal of Child Psychology and Psychiatry*, Vol. 39, No. 4, 1998, pp. 465-76.

15 Fergusson, D.M., Lynskey, M. and Horwood, L.J., 'The adolescent outcomes of adoption: a 16-year longitudinal study', *Journal of Child Psychology and Psychiatry*, Vol. 36, No. 4, 1995, pp. 597-615.

16 Hetherington, E.M. and Stanley-Hagan, M. (reviewing the impacts of divorce research), 'The adjustment of children with divorced parents: a risk and resiliency perspective', *Journal of Child Psychology and Psychiatry*, Vol. 40, No. 1, 1999, pp. 129-40.

17 Fergusson, Lynskey and Horwood, *Journal of Child Psychology and Psychiatry*, *op. cit.*

18 Fagan, *Why Serious Welfare Must Include Serious Adoption Reform, op. cit.*; Maughan, Collishaw and Pickles, *Journal of Child Psychology and Psychiatry, op. cit.*

19 Ministerial Group on the Family, *Supporting Families: A Consultation Document*, London: Stationery Office, November 1998.

20 Morgan, *Adoption and the Care of Children, op. cit.*, pp. 136, 154.

21 It is a sad commentary that the British Agencies for Adoption and Fostering, from its skewed experience of post-adoption cases, has over recent years been somewhat lukewarm concerning the adoption option. Too often BAAF has seemed part of the ideological problem rather than enthusiastic about the early securing of children's identities; and it could have done far more both to publicise the studies of successful outcomes from adoptions in time past, and to credit the work of many placement agencies which operated excellent procedural systems when adoption was more in vogue.

22 Dr James Appleyard, Chairman, British Medical Association's Working Group on Child Health, upon the launch of the BMA Report, *Growing Up in Britian*, London: 30 June 1999.

23 See further, in summary, Whitfield, R., *Security of Attachment: A Necessary Objective in Taking Ourselves and Children Seriously*, Annual Review of St George's House, Windsor Castle, 1996, pp. 81-91.

Index

IEA Health and Welfare Unit

Independence

The Health and Welfare Unit is part of the Institute of Economic Affairs, a registered educational charity (No. 235351) founded in 1955. Like the IEA, the Health and Welfare Unit is financed from a variety of private sources to avoid over-reliance on any single or small group of donors.

All IEA publications are independently refereed and referees' comments are passed on anonymously to authors. The IEA gratefully acknowledges the contributions made to its educational work by the eminent scholars who act as referees.

All the Institute's publications seek to further its objective of promoting the advancement of learning, by research into economic and political science, by education of the public therein, and by the dissemination of ideas, research and the results of research in these subjects. The views expressed are those of the authors, not of the IEA, which has no corporate view.

THE INSTITUTE OF ECONOMIC AFFAIRS